# Birmingham

Edited by Annabel Cook

 Young**Writers**

First published in Great Britain in 2007 by:
Young Writers
Remus House
Coltsfoot Drive
Peterborough
PE2 9JX
Telephone: 01733 890066
Website: www.youngwriters.co.uk

SB ISBN 978-1 84602 963 9

# Foreword

Young Writers was established in 1991 and has been passionately devoted to the promotion of reading and writing in children and young adults ever since. The quest continues today. Young Writers remains as committed to the nurturing of poetic and literary talent as ever.

This year's Young Writers competition has proven as vibrant and dynamic as ever and we are delighted to present a showcase of the best poetry from across the UK and in some cases overseas. Each poem has been selected from a wealth of *Little Laureates* entries before ultimately being published in this, our sixteenth primary school poetry series.

Once again, we have been supremely impressed by the overall quality of the entries we have received. The imagination, energy and creativity which has gone into each young writer's entry made choosing the poems a challenging and often difficult but ultimately hugely rewarding task - the general high standard of the work submitted ensured this opportunity to bring their poetry to a larger appreciative audience.

We sincerely hope you are pleased with this final collection and that you will enjoy *Little Laureates Birmingham* for many years to come.

# Contents

Charis Hunter-Rice  (9)                                      17
Lauren Jones  (8)                                           17
Joshua Wykes  (9)                                          18
Kelsey Ross  (8)                                           18
Luke Bracken  (8)                                          19
Ambah Ellis  (9)                                           19
Ben Welch  (9)                                             20
Charlotte Foxall  (9)                                      20
Joseph Welch  (9)                                          21
Katie Lackey  (9)                                          21
Jessica Ward  (9)                                          22
Abigail Taylor  (9)                                        22
Felica Greenfield  (8)                                     23
Kirsty Oliver  (8)                                         23
Jordan Hawkins  (8)                                        24
James Rudd  (9)                                            24
Megan Searle  (8)                                          25
Chloe Underwood  (9)                                       25
Johnathon Hawthorn  (9)                                    26
Elli Layland  (8)                                          26
Charlotte Greenley  (8)                                    27
Mitchell Smith  (9)                                        27
Tamara Lord  (9)                                           28
Luke Malkin  (8)                                           28
Laura Bicknell  (9)                                        29
Dean Morgan  (9)                                           29
Rachael Finnerty  (9)                                      30
Meena Ali  (8)                                             30
Renée Blissett  (8)                                        31
Thomas Lissemore  (9)                                      31
James Ricketts  (9)                                        32
Simon Eccles  (8)                                          32
Reiss Munslow  (8)                                         32
Callum Ward  (8)                                           33
Ronan Sheehan  (8)                                         33
Demi Roberts  (8)                                          34
Callum Gander  (9)                                         35

**Hawkesley Church Primary School**
Caitlan Hall  (7)                                          35
Deanna Arlington  (8)                                      35

| | |
|---|---|
| Rebekah Hare  (8) | 36 |
| Kalum McCrea  (8) | 36 |
| Chantelle Quinn  (8) | 36 |
| Jodie Chandler  (9) | 37 |
| Lauren Robertson  (10) | 37 |
| Michael Henderson  (9) | 37 |
| Kayleigh Shirley  (9) | 38 |
| Kaleigh Astbury  (7) | 38 |
| Usmaan Ali  (9) | 38 |
| Charity Bravington  (9) | 39 |
| Chloe Butcher  (8) | 39 |
| Chloe Welsh  (8) | 39 |
| Jade Sykes  (10) | 40 |
| Liam Fendick  (9) | 40 |
| Nayer Caesar  (7) | 40 |
| Joshua Harrington  (9) | 41 |
| Chloe Smith  (10) | 41 |
| Hannah Horton  (8) | 41 |
| Sian Kelly  (10) | 42 |
| Rebecca Wincott  (8) | 42 |
| Dean Hensey  (9) | 42 |
| Chloe Jones  (10) | 43 |
| Paige Britton  (9) | 43 |
| Shelby Barrington-Smith  (10) | 43 |
| Remi Graham  (9) | 44 |
| Kyanne Brookes  (10) | 44 |
| Yasmin Harvey  (9) | 45 |
| Amy Coggins  (10) | 45 |
| Kielo Brown  (10) | 46 |
| Chloe Maddocks  (9) | 46 |

## James Brindley Children's Hospital
| | |
|---|---|
| Hannah Prentice  (11) | 47 |
| Angelo Evangelou  (10) | 47 |
| Millie Hodson Walker (7) | 47 |
| Amaanat Hussain  (10) | 48 |

## Leigh Junior, Infant & Nursery School
| | |
|---|---|
| Mohammed Arslan  (10) | 48 |
| Hassan Hussain  (10) | 49 |
| Shafan Mohammed  (9) | 49 |

| | |
|---|---|
| Naila Abid  (10) | 50 |
| Tayba Nawaz  (10) | 50 |
| Aliya Balal  (9) | 50 |
| Marieh Parveen  (10) | 51 |

## Lyndon Green Junior School

| | |
|---|---|
| Amy Ellis  (8) | 51 |
| Chloe Bond  (7) | 52 |
| Ryan French  (9) | 52 |
| Joshua Preece  (9) | 53 |
| Megan Goodwin  (8) | 53 |
| Abigail Jones  (9) | 53 |
| Emma Warwood  (10) | 54 |
| Bethan Machray  (10) | 54 |
| Demi Baker  (8) | 54 |
| Isobel Wattison  (9) | 55 |
| Lauren Boyle  (8) | 55 |

## Oaklands Primary School

| | |
|---|---|
| Louise Doherty  (10) | 56 |
| Aqeela Zafar  (11) | 56 |
| Laura Chui  (10) | 57 |
| Sufyaan Zafar  (9) | 57 |
| Lauren Gilligan  (9) | 58 |
| Grace Verona  (9) | 58 |
| Kathryn Hope  (11) | 59 |
| Sarah Keating  (10) | 59 |

## Robin Hood J&I NC School

| | |
|---|---|
| Alanna Ayres  (10) | 60 |
| Joshua Ryder  (10) | 60 |
| Charlotte Winder  (9) | 61 |
| Bina Lakha  (11) | 61 |
| Tahrif Khan  (10) | 62 |
| Rachel Batten  (9) | 62 |
| Jaspreet Bhogal  (9) | 63 |
| Jack Sandall  (11) | 63 |
| Alex Phelan  (10) | 64 |
| Joe Hinckes  (11) | 64 |
| Muhammad Azarpay  (11) | 65 |
| Sonal Gohil  (10) | 65 |

| | |
|---|---|
| Anthony Briggs  (9) | 66 |
| Sabrina Bano  (10) | 66 |
| Haroon Gulfraz  (10) | 67 |
| Javeria Khan  (11) | 67 |
| Rahim Azimul  (10) | 68 |
| Jordan Golding  (11) | 68 |
| Manisha Kaur  (11) | 69 |
| Keval Vadukul  (11) | 69 |
| Wasim Ahmed  (11) | 70 |
| Nicholas Wall  (10) | 70 |
| Isidora Mazibrada  (10) | 71 |
| Hatim Hassanali  (9) | 71 |
| Aqsa Ahmed  (10) | 72 |
| Katy Griffiths  (10) | 73 |
| Sam Muxlow  (11) | 74 |
| Anastasia Raw  (9) | 75 |
| Dilan Chauhan  (10) | 75 |
| Sam Covill  (9) | 75 |
| Vishaal Dhokiya  (11) | 76 |

### St Catherine of Siena RC Primary School, Lee Bank

| | |
|---|---|
| Chantelle Swain  (9) | 76 |
| Alisha Ullah  (10) | 77 |
| Naomi-Sarah Donaldson  (9) | 78 |
| Laura Payne  (11) | 78 |
| Chanice Hepburn  (10) | 79 |
| Aaron Reiss Parmar  (10) | 79 |
| Jamilah Mohammed  (8) | 79 |

### St James' CE Primary School, Handsworth

| | |
|---|---|
| Eshe Mwilima  (10) | 80 |
| Megan Sagal  (9) | 80 |
| Nikita Janagil  (11) | 81 |
| Andrew McIntosh  (8) | 81 |
| Paul Fisher  (10) | 82 |
| Hashim Khurram  (9) | 82 |
| Arrandeep Dhillon  (l10) | 83 |
| Dana Fisher  (8) | 83 |
| Bisma Mughal  (9) | 84 |
| Jothi Najran  (9) | 84 |

## Stirchley Community School

| | |
|---|---|
| Nathan Bayliss  (10) | 85 |
| Kyle Kemp  (9) | 85 |
| Gary Cooper  (11) | 85 |
| James Beck  (11) | 86 |
| Daniel Peel  (10) | 86 |
| Jared Pellow  (10) | 86 |
| Shannon McCleary  (9) | 87 |
| Abrar Chowdhury  (10) | 87 |
| Martin West  (10) | 87 |
| Emma Jones  (10) | 88 |
| Kain Aldred-Barnett  (10) | 88 |
| John Ford  (10) | 88 |
| Jarobi Lorenzo-Whervin  (10) | 89 |
| Akram Azad  (10) | 89 |
| Sam Tanner  (9) | 89 |
| Hollie Shakespeare  (11) | 90 |
| Bethany Caldicott  (10) | 90 |
| Monica Gregory  (10) | 90 |
| Tiar Baxter  (10) | 91 |
| Martin Frankland  (10) | 91 |
| Toby Traylen  (10) | 91 |
| Leah Chitiyo  (11) | 92 |
| Amy McWilliams  (10) | 92 |
| George Garvie  (11) | 92 |
| Shaun Caldicott  (10) | 93 |
| Idei Durose  (10) | 93 |
| Nicole Evans  (9) | 93 |
| Aqeelah Ali  (10) | 94 |

## Topcliffe J&I School

| | |
|---|---|
| Jade Griffiths  (10) | 94 |
| Laura Green  (11) | 95 |
| Hannah Jones  (10) | 95 |
| Annemarie Johnson  (10) | 96 |
| Ellie O'Brien  (9) | 96 |
| Aimee Lee  (10) | 97 |
| Ben Selby  (10) | 97 |
| Kimberley Banner  (10) | 97 |

# Whitecrest Primary School

| | |
|---|---|
| Lauren Gillespie  (9) | 98 |
| Katie Beddows  (7) | 98 |
| Lauren Middleton  (8) | 99 |
| Arjun Sangha  (8) | 99 |
| Hema Moor  (7) | 100 |
| Eleanor Kumar  (8) | 100 |
| Libby Randall  (7) | 101 |
| Chloe Pickard  (9) | 101 |
| Max Purcell-Burrows  (11) | 102 |
| Coral Hatfield  (9) | 102 |
| Rhys Williams  (11) | 103 |
| Owen Morris  (7) | 103 |
| Brittany Cox  (9) | 104 |
| Jagjit Padham  (9) | 104 |
| Saprina Moor  (11) | 105 |
| Emma Barker  (8) | 105 |
| Cara Harrigan  (10) | 106 |
| Thomas Aston  (7) | 106 |
| Katie Lunn  (10) | 107 |
| Jake Wood  (8) | 107 |
| Thomas Farr  (8) | 108 |
| Harry Watts  (8) | 108 |
| Gurdylan Sanghera  (8) | 108 |
| Leigh Burton  (9) | 109 |
| Gabriel Bradnick  (9) | 109 |
| Matthew Watt  (10) | 110 |
| Jake Simkiss  (10) | 110 |
| Lauren Manton  (11) | 111 |

# The Poems

# Birthday Gift

There are things I'd like to say
To you, my love, on a special day.
I am forever thankful God sent you my way.
Like a gift from above
You showed me how it is to feel real love.
I know how many mountains we've had to climb
And how forever it seemed for a very long time.
Yes, we have endured our share of pain
But together we have so much to gain.
Bigger mountains may lie ahead
But together there is no hill we cannot tread.
So always remember my love for you
And there is nothing together we can do.
I'll be here forever, my love is true,
The person beside me, that would be you.

**Sardara Singh Narotra  (8)**
Acocks Green Primary School


# My Week, My Life

Every day I walk to school,
I use the Green Cross Code
Which is very cool.

When I reach the playground
I find my friends
And we have a run around.

When the lessons start,
I listen and learn
So I will grow up to be very smart.

Football's my game when the weekend comes,
I put on my Bromford Lions' kit
Cos we are the champions.

**Jason Sutton  (7)**
Acocks Green Primary School

# Everyone Needs A Friend

When you need a shoulder to cry on,
Remember that I have a warm embrace,
Ready to offer you comfort.

When you think I'm being too tough,
Remember that which does not kill you makes you stronger.

When you need a friend to listen,
Remember that I am here for you always.

When you doubt me, remember,
And when you lose faith in yourself,
Remember that I never did, nor ever will.

I dig for memories
In the gardens in my mind,
But seeds of dreams that never grew

Are all I ever find,
And it's all so long ago,
And it's all too close,

And as I kneel before you,
I hope this will end,

Because I'm tired and lonely
And I just want my friend.

**Sohail Suleman (8)**
**Acocks Green Primary School**

# Flowers

Flowers are beautiful,
Flowers are divine,
Flowers need water,
Flowers need sunshine,
Flowers are sweet-smelling,
Flowers are like you and me,
I wish there could be flowers everywhere we be!
Flowers have pollen,
Flowers have nectar,
Flowers have seeds,
Which all of us can nearly see!
Flowers help the world,
Flowers help us,
Can you imagine a world without any flowers?

**Santkaur Narotra (11)**
**Acocks Green Primary School**


# I Dream

I dream of being a pop star but it never quite works out
So I bring out my frizzy hairbrush and start wiggling about
My mum and dad they always say it just is not my time
And then I'll come out with some silly words that don't even rhyme.
My dad with the tapping foot, my mum with that annoying little tut,
Even my brother has his hands on his face,
'Oh my gosh, what's happening in this place?'
But you just wait; you just wait and see,
I will be a pop star in a year . . . or three!

**Autumn Dennis-Stephens (9)**
**Acocks Green Primary School**

# Who Is God?

God is our great leader,
He is also our feeder.
He gives us food and money,
He tries to make our day sunny.
We pray to God every day.
'You are the best,' we say.

God is always there for us,
Just like that, there is no fuss.
We should give God the right respect,
The respect that we always expect.

God has made us who we are,
Not on the inside, not on the outside.
No matter how you look,
Or how you talk or what you wear,
Remember that God is everywhere.
No one can change that.

**Natasha Ghani  (11)**
**Benson Community School**


# Love

Love is me,
Love is you,
Love is the way it should be.
Without love in the world
There would be no peace and harmony.
Love is the feeling that we all feel,
Love is understanding that we should share,
Love is the feeling that is getting so rare.

**Rozeta Kumari  (11)**
**Benson Community School**

# The Mental Mind Bully

The mental mind bully,
He follows me absolutely everywhere.
When I close my tired, weary eyes,
He's always there, unwilling to go and let me sleep.
The mental mind bully.

Tick-tock, the menacing sound of the clock,
Time's running out says the clock,
The bully's coming for you,
You can't escape it,
It's all your fault!

The mind bully,
He's always there and I don't think I can take it much more,
He criticises when there is nothing to criticise,
I know he's only in my mind,
But it feels so constant!

I feel like he's always there, punching and battering my brain,
He doesn't even really exist
And it's all because of the horror movies
And my obsession with watching them.

But it's going to be OK now,
I have a special doctor
Who can help me get over my fears,
And now that bully is out of here.

**Aaliyah Burgher  (10)**
**Benson Community School**

## About A Beautiful Girl

All the special happiness
A lovely girl brings . . .
Moments filled with sunshine
And all your
Favourite things . . .

All the joy a year can hold and
Every dream comes true,
These are the girls
Wishes made
Especially for you.

**Renee Lorde-Samuels (11)**
Benson Community School


## Seashell

Seashell at my ear,
What do I hear?
The calming sounds of the sea.

The waves lash and fall
As the sea roars
And then come calming sighs.

**Divya Kaur Chote (10)**
Benson Community School


## The Snail

I am small and friendly,
I like to eat delicious, juicy grass and brown leaves.
I do not bite and I am soft.
I leave trails behind me,
But people don't see me and tread on me.
I am that small but my friends live in flowers
And I live under loads of rocks.

**Ellesse Moran-Nabi (9)**
Bordesley Village Primary School

# Apple

I am juicy, delicious,
Yummy and scrumptious
And I am the only one left.
I am a fruit,
I am not a normal fruit,
I am a delicious fruit.
I wonder who is going to eat me?
You can get lots of apples on an apple tree,
But no one is as juicy, delicious,
Yummy and scrumptious as me.
Yummy!

**Farwah Shah  (10)**
**Bordesley Village Primary School**


# Star

I looked up at the starry sky,
There you were, a bright little star
Twinkling on your very own.
I can watch you all night long.
How you look so far away,
Make my troubles go away.
How I wish you could stay,
Sprinkle some magic dust on me
So I can be a magical sparkling star like you.
Forever together we will be
Two twinkling, shiny, happy, bright stars.

**Haleema Mahallah  (9)**
**Bordesley Village Primary School**

# Ways Of Looking At The Sky

The different shades of blue
Amongst the clouds,
As if it were new,
But it has always been there.

Gets blocked by the evilness,
The whiteness and the dark,
The blueness is the best,
But the evil goes aside.

It makes the sea turn blue,
But sometimes it is clear,
Having had this too,
They're the same thing.

It is the lungs of the world,
If it wasn't there, then we wouldn't be here,
It's on the breathing mode,
It helps us just the same.

Like a blanket of stars
Keeping it bright,
Which are so very far,
Helping us helpfully.

The sun is up,
The moon is down,
The moon is up,
The sun is down.

It would be grey and dull unless
It was there every day,
Keeping everything the same.
We don't see it like others do.

**Joseph Oakes (10)**
**Cotteridge JI School**

# Ways Of Looking At A Flower

Underneath our footsteps
Lies a little seed,
Who knows what it will become,
Flower, bush or weed?

Now a sprout bursts through the earth,
The seeds begin to grow,
This will soon become a stem
With roots spreading below.

Now grow the buds
That get ready to open,
The plant has grown leaves
And spring has begun.

Now the bud opens
And you can see its head.
There are beautiful colours,
A rainbow on a flower bed.

The pollen in the centre
Makes it smell so sweet,
Who knows what insects
This flower may meet?

First comes an ant
And then comes a bee,
Who carries the pollen
When it sticks to his knee.

They shelter all insects,
They give them homes too,
They are lovely to look at
For me and for you.

**Sophie Yates  (11)**
**Cotteridge JI School**

# Ways Of Looking At Endangered Animals

Elephants may squirt you with water
But that does not give the right to slaughter.

Gorillas beat their chests as hard as they can
But that is stopping for the right of Man.

Pandas love their bamboo
But the bamboo is dying and the pandas are too.

Rhinos come in black and white
But more and more do not see the light.

The polar bears love the snow
But the bears seem to come and go.

The tiger is the biggest cat ever
But who will remember after they have gone forever?

Birds rule the sky
But that is stopping as more die.

We know all of God's creatures' names
So why should we stop their amazing fame?

They rule the sea, sky and land,
It is like we should be under their command.

They keep our world alive
So do not let them run and hide.

Even if they're all alone
Remember they have lives of their own.

They may be wild and crazy
But we are worse - we are lazy!

From the meat-eaters to the leaf-eaters
They keep our planet alive.

**Sam Hughes  (10)**
**Cotteridge JI School**

# Ways Of Looking At A Tree

The giant stands here
All alone
Not doing any harm
With all its charms.

Their great waving arms
Welcome animals
To their home
For a comfy stay.

The animals feel safe
In its great big body
Warm and cosy.

While we are having fun
Trees all over the world
Are dying.

People use trees as graffiti walls
As the tree stands there getting ruined
Everything the tree does for us
And doesn't even get a thank you.

Of all the homes it provides
Animals don't even ask,
The tree never gets a thank you
No one knows that the tree cries.

The tree makes paper
For us to use
Then we give the tree abuse.

Helps our environment
Here and there
All we give it is a scare.

**Emma Parker  (11)**
**Cotteridge JI School**

# Ways Of Looking At God

He made everything and everyone,
He made us all alive,
Every animal and creature,
Even stinging bees in their hive.

*Chorus*
God where are you?
God where can you be?
God I need you,
Can't you see?

God is everywhere,
Night and day,
He tucks us in at night,
But never goes away.

*Chorus*

He must have been sad,
All alone with no one,
Then He made us
And His loneliness was gone.

*Chorus*

He is kind to everything,
It's like He's the air,
He never fusses or anything,
But people pretend He's not there.

*Chorus*

God is there, the kindest thing,
He'll never complain,
Even though there are mean people
That take His name in vain.

*Chorus*

God gives us everything,
But we don't know the reasons.
He gave all the things,
Even different seasons.

*Chorus.*

**Josephine Smith   (10)**
Cotteridge JI School


# Ways Of Looking At A Tree

Trees are very wise
All the way up so tall
Their big branch eyes
Look down at you who are very small

Its firewood keeps you warm
Nice and dry too
Until the early dawn

The tree up there so high
Here I live under your branch
So why do you die?

If it was not for you
Then who would keep me alive?
Why are we killing you?

I look at you in spring
And all I see
Are beautiful colours
So you cheer me up

I lie on you at night
The base of my bed
Is made from you
For my head hits it
For your body it's alive

People live in you
But who is killing you?

**Rebecca Ramsay   (11)**
Cotteridge JI School

# Ways Of Looking At Sound

Sound is all around us,
Different pitches: high, low,
And different volumes: loud and quiet.
We hear it through vibrations
Just like a deer hearing its calf crying for its mother.
Sound will echo forever
Like people gently playing pianos.

Sound is everywhere,
Like God watching our every move.

The sound of the birds singing in the morning
When you open the curtains to watch them
And the voice of your mum when she calls you for your tea,
And the sound of the laughter infants make when you chase them,
The sound of the Christmas crackers when you sit down for lunch
                              with your family,
Or even the sound of someone lighting a match.
These are some of my favourite sounds.

**Bethan Robinson  (11)**
Cotteridge JI School


# Ways Of Looking At The Earth

The sky made of shades of blue,
The sea like a sapphire going on forever, freely and vast,
Emerald-green leaves dancing in the breeze,
Trees whispering to one another,
Volcanoes, like a person angered, ready to erupt any second,
These are all elements of the Earth, the only planet with life,
People take it for granted but know that nothing lasts forever.
People walk on Earth every day yet their eyes are blind to the
                              beauty and secrets it holds.
Can we wake up from this nightmare of destroying the rainforest
                              and littering?
Can we come to our senses and realise all we need is here?
The Earth, it stands out above all the other planets
Like the most colourful flower in the flower bed.

**Myles Labhaya  (11)**
Cotteridge JI School

# Horses

Horses like grass,
Flowers,
Hay,
Stables,
Water,
Straw,
And they neigh.

**Nathan Travis  (10)**
Forest Oak Special School


# Horses

Horses eat hay
And you can ride them every day.
They are big
And their hair looks like a wig.

**Brittany Langley  (11)**
Forest Oak Special School


# What Am I?

The greatest gorilla of them all
Lives in his tree and swings like a hyperactive sloth.
And when he's on the floor,
Gallops better than a horse.

What am I?

When it's fighting for the crown,
Its teeth are bigger than a clown.
When it's mated
It climbs to the top of its tree.

Have a guess?

**Elliott Hill  (9)**
Glenmead Primary School

# My Animal Poem

My dog can bark happy and loud,
Like a tall, skinny greyhound,
Joyful as can be,
Wagging her tail in front of me.
Chasing all the little cats,
Not getting dressed in silly hats.

Walking quietly along the street,
Trying to find rubbish to eat.
Running around with bones in her mouth,
Running around all on the grass
With all those flowers that go past.

She's very tired at the end of the day,
Because she's always trying to get other dogs' prey.
Falling asleep on the sofa,
Always getting me into trouble
By letting her up for a little cuddle.

**Gemma Malkin (8)**
Glenmead Primary School

# Save Our Planet

Animals could die if we keep cutting down trees.
Bad pollution makes smoke, smoke makes asthma.
Cars, too many cars using loads of fuel.
Don't put rubbish in the sea or on top of a hill.
Never use too much electricity, turn it off.
Flowers should be treated more nicely.
Global warming should be gone, it can't though.
However, don't throw paper, *recycle.*
If you want to do vandalism, *don't.*

**Edward Shakespeare (8)**
Glenmead Primary School

# Save Our Planet

Do you walk everywhere you go
Even though it is so slow?
In the mornings do you walk to school?
Walking is the perfect tool!
It wakes you up, it makes you ready!
Don't go fast, take it steady!

Do you recycle,
Or do you put things in the bin?
If you recycle, you'll always win!
Did you know rubbish stays on Earth forever?
It does! It won't go! Never, never, never!

Turn off the tap when you do your teeth,
Save the fish swimming in a reef.
So save some water, save the Earth,
You'll thank me for all it's worth.

**Charis Hunter-Rice  (9)**
**Glenmead Primary School**


# Colours Of The Rainbow

Red is the bright red petals of a rose
For a Valentine to love.
Orange is the form of the sun
That shines so bright on metal.
Yellow is the middle of the candle flame
That helps us to see in dark places.
Green is the very top of a tree
That waves and whistles in the wind.
Blue is the masses of sea
That waves and crashes on rocks and stones.
Violet is the top of a bluebell
That tries to reach the top of the trees.

**Lauren Jones  (8)**
**Glenmead Primary School**

# My Alphabet

A is for animals scattering around,
   save their plants or they will die.
B is for buildings, don't
   knock them down.
C is for composting,
   growing more things.
D is for diseases
   making people ill.
E is for electricity, wasting it
   to watch boring soaps.
F is for factories giving
   away pollution.
G is for global warming
   melting away the snow.
H is for historical buildings,
   we knocked them down to build fat supermarkets.

**Joshua Wykes (9)**
Glenmead Primary School


# The Rainbow

Red is . . . the scent of roses
Which blossom every spring.

Orange is . . . the look of the sun setting
As it slowly fades away.

Yellow is . . . the juice of a lemon
That starts to tingle on my tongue.

Green is . . . the leaves on a tree
That sway in the breeze.

Blue is . . . the waves of the sea
That glisten on the shore.

Black is . . . the look of onyx
That shines in the light.

**Kelsey Ross (8)**
Glenmead Primary School

# The Future

What will be
Left here for me
When I grow up?

Litter is rotting our streets,
It can kill small animals.

Will there be
Bins to put
Litter inside?

Will there be
Animals for meat,
Making our bones stronger?

Will there be
More land
Than there was before?

**Luke Bracken (8)**
**Glenmead Primary School**


# Colours All Around

Red is . . . the juice of an apple
Crunching away in your mouth.

Orange is . . . the burn of the sun
Burning away and making things light.

Yellow is . . . the brightness of a light
Shining in your bedroom.

Green is . . . the sweetness of a grape
Making you dribble while you eat it.

Blue is . . . the scent of the bluebell
Filling the room with a sweet smell.

Violet is . . . the silk of a top
Making you feel like a flower.

**Ambah Ellis (9)**
**Glenmead Primary School**

# My Future

What will be left for me
When I grow up?

Will pollution rise and leave?
Will it make it hard to breathe?

Will litter rot the roads?
What if it makes toads?

Will the food be fresh to eat?
Will diseases catch the meat?

Water is running out,
Soon the rivers will be
Nothing but dirt.

The world is getting hot,
But it's something we can't stop.

Will the animals still survive
Or will they become extinct?

**Ben Welch  (9)**
Glenmead Primary School


# The Rainbow Poem

Red is . . . the runny blood
Running down your hand.

Orange is . . . the glow of the sun
Glowing in the sunset.

Yellow is . . . the brightness of the sand
Burning your feet as you walk across it.

Green is . . . the sweetness of an apple
As you bite into it.

Blue is . . . the waves of the sea
Banging at the rocks by the lighthouse.

Violet is . . . the prettiness of a flower
In the field, swaying in the wind.

**Charlotte Foxall  (9)**
Glenmead Primary School

# My Colour Poems

Red is . . . the heart of a fire,
Romantic roses all to desire.

Red is . . . the outskirts of the sun,
Watch out, it's on the run.

Red is . . . the living of blood,
To keep us living the way we should.

Black is . . . dark in the night,
Oh, what a marvellous sight.

Black is . . . the black of a chalkboard,
Don't write with chalk so broad.

Black is . . . the beauty of a limousine,
My mom's curious, I think she's keen.

Blue is . . . the light of the sky,
It doesn't talk, it must be shy.

**Joseph Welch  (9)**
**Glenmead Primary School**


# Pandas' Lifestyle

Pandas here, pandas there,
Pandas everywhere.
Climbing trees, chasing bees,
Breaking branches to and fro.

Branches snapping out of control,
Twigs broken here and there,
Pulling their legs to climb a tree.

Pandas munching but never to be seen,
Loud and quiet, where have they been?

Bamboo crunching as they go,
Rustling, cracking and snapping twigs
Through the trees of bamboo.

**Katie Lackey  (9)**
**Glenmead Primary School**

# Colours!

Red is . . . the burning of a fire
That burns fiercely on Bonfire Night.

Orange is . . . the brightness of a beautiful sunset
That makes an eye-catching view.

Yellow is . . . the glisten of the sun,
It glistens all day long.

Green is . . . the sparkle of an emerald
That sparkles on a cosy cushion.

Blue is . . . the wavy sea,
The waves are blue and calm.

Indigo is . . . the denim of jeans,
Shades of different coloured denim.

Violet is . . . the prettiness of a blossom,
The petals falling off in autumn.

Brown is . . . the dullness of bricks.
Builders use them to make houses.

White is . . . the dryness of some flowers,
Standing tall and brightening up your room.

**Jessica Ward (9)**
**Glenmead Primary School**


# What Animal Am I?

He squeaks and squawks very loud,
He eats his mix of dry food,
Slowly he always runs
Around his hutch
Like some wild cheetah,
Kicking and scratching all the time.
Drinks and slurps his water
And he sleeps very quietly.
What animal is he?

**Abigail Taylor (9)**
**Glenmead Primary School**

# Pink, Blue And Red

*Pink*
Pink is my cat's collar, pulling lightly.
Pink is the yummy ice cream tasting deliciously nice.
Pink is the bright paint dribbling down my wall.
Pink is the colour of lipstick smudging on my cheeks.
Pink is the colour of a pig rolling in dirty mud.

*Blue*
Blue is the colour of the beautiful sky gazing at the yellow sun.
Blue is the colour of berries shining in my garden.
Blue is a dolphin swimming in the beautiful sea.
Blue is the colour of the laptop I work on.
Blue is the colour of my wallpaper.

*Red*
Red is the colour of a hairband shining in the sun.
Red is the colour of my lips shining at night.
Red is the colour of my sharpener, big and beautiful.
Red is the colour of strawberries sitting in a pile.
Red is the colour of apples, juicy and sweet.

**Felica Greenfield  (8)**
Glenmead Primary School


# My Poem

Blue is like the sea,
The waves crashing on the beach.
Blue is like forget-me-nots,
Growing in the soil.
Blue is like ice, cold and chilly.
Blue is like sky, bright in the daylight.

Red is like fire, brightens up the air.
Red is like blood that flows through your body.
Red is like nail varnish, shimmers on my nails.
Red is like lobster, that is my favourite food.

**Kirsty Oliver  (8)**
Glenmead Primary School

# Colours

*Green*
Green is a sports car zooming quickly down the road.
Green is a shiny apple shining brightly on a tree.
Green is a banana up high and unripe in a swaying tree.
Green is juicy bubblegum which you blow a big and smooth
bubble with.

*Red*
Red is a ring shining brightly in the sun.
Red is a Ferrari speeding down a racing track.
Red is a ball bouncing up and down.
Red is a swimming ring floating happily in the water.

*Blue*
Blue is a dinosaur roaring happily in the shining sun.
Blue is a bottle ready to fizz coldly out.
Blue is a motorbike speeding down the road.
Blue is a shark hunting for fish.

**Jordan Hawkins  (8)**
Glenmead Primary School


# My Animal

My animal pounces and runs and leaps
And climbs, it does lots of things,
And when it runs quickly and is ready to pounce,
A human being will not stand a chance.

Quickly and quietly it creeps and looks for its prey.
Sometimes it fights or plays,
And when it fights, don't go close,
It might bite.

It pounces very high, it's got to be careful.
When it leaps, it can grip on trees, climb and sleep.
When it sleeps, it purrs and sleeps quietly.
What's my animal?

*A: A cheetah.*

**James Rudd  (9)**
Glenmead Primary School

# Colours

*Red*
Red is a springtime rose blooming in the sun.
Red is a sweet cherry, delicious to taste.
Red is as juicy as bubblegum, like your lips.
Red is a fire engine zooming for an emergency.

*Brown*
Brown is like a pig rolling happily in the mud.
Brown is as creamy as a chocolate bar.
Brown is as wavy as brown curly hair.
Brown is a pen that flows across the page.

*Yellow*
Yellow is as bright as the yellow sun.
Yellow is as soft as a yellow banana.
Yellow is as comfy as a yellow pillow.
Yellow is as new as a spring dandelion.

**Megan Searle (8)**
Glenmead Primary School

# My Colour Poem!

Gold is the cup we hardly win.
Gold is the deep sand tickling my bare toes.
Gold is the long flowers rising in the garden.
Gold is my teddy, so soft and cuddly.

Red is a ruby, as shiny as can be.
Red is a flame of a fire, so bright and warm.
Red is an apple, so crunchy and sweet.
Red is my cat's collar, so they know she's not a stray.

Blue is the sky, as bright as can be.
Blue is ice, so chilly and cold.
Blue is bluebells that I only see in spring.
Blue is the dolphin jumping gently in the sea.

**Chloe Underwood (9)**
Glenmead Primary School

# My Poem

*Brown*
Brown are the pegs wobbling on the tight washing line.
Brown is the fur of bears that jump and kill.
Brown is the drawing neatly done.
Brown is the soft sand shining in the bright sun.

*White*
White is a car that zooms down the road.
White is the snow, clear and bright.
White is the paint dripping down the wall.
White is a rubber, rubbing out messy work.

*Blue*
Blue is Chelsea scoring beautiful goals.
Blue is the sky, clean and nice.
Blue is the river smoothly going along.
Blue is a coat, cosy and warm.

**Johnathon Hawthorn  (9)**
Glenmead Primary School


# Colours

Blue is the sky, a colour of an eye.
Blue is the Villa shirt shining bright in the sky.
Blue is a folder holding pages of work.

Red is a fire engine saving people from bad fright.
Red is the colour of blood running around your body day and night.
Red are lips that talk all day, they will move and say.

Yellow is the colour of a banana that you eat every day.
Yellow is the colour of the moon and stars, near and far.
Yellow is the colour of the sun shining bright in the sky.
Yellow is the colour of the McDonald's sign high in the sky.

**Elli Layland  (8)**
Glenmead Primary School

# White, Red And Blue

*White*
White is fur of a polar bear sleeping on the cold ice.
White is the colour of the fluffy cloud in the sky.
White is the paper, clear and bright.
White is the snowdrops falling lightly from the sky.

*Red*
Red is the colour of the kissing lips.
Red is the colour of a flowing scarf.
Red is the colour of the panda running up the big tree.
Red is the apple so juicy and sweet.

*Blue*
Blue is the colour of the bright sky.
Blue is the colour of a car that goes smoothly.
Blue is the colour of the dazzling sea.
Blue is the colour of the laptop, shining so light.

**Charlotte Greenley  (8)**
Glenmead Primary School

# Colours

Blue is my car zooming down the mountain.
Blue is the sky, so bright and clear.
Blue is my coat which keeps me warm.
Blue is ice, so slippy and slidey.

Red is blood which runs through your veins.
Red is roses that wave in the wind.
Red is a strawberry which tastes delicious.
Red is a berry, so sweet and sour.

Yellow is the sun which brightens up the Earth.
Yellow is the colour of a banana that I love to eat.
Yellow is my maths book which I work in.
Yellow is my car which I drive.

**Mitchell Smith  (9)**
Glenmead Primary School

# Colours

Red is . . . the juice of a strawberry running down your chin.
Red is . . . the heart of a fire keeping you warm in winter.
Red is . . . the romance of a rose in someone's hand on
Valentine's Day.
Orange is . . . the gloss of the sunset, drifting away at the end of
the day.
Orange is . . . the fruit that I love the most.
Orange is . . . the sand of a hot desert making you thirsty as you
walk along.
Yellow is . . . the colour of the fruit that is sour.
Yellow is . . . the quack of a duck which you feed with bread at
the park.

**Tamara Lord (9)**
Glenmead Primary School


# Colours

Blue is the car zooming down the road.
Blue are the eyes that sparkle really bright.
Blue are the gloves that keep my hands warm.
Blue are the lights that sparkle on the Christmas tree.

Green is the grass that grows up high.
Green are the frogs that *ribbet* on the lily pads.
Green is the paint that makes my house colourful.
Green is the limeade that I drink.

Orange is the paint that colours my house.
Orange is the hair that makes me look good.
Orange is the top that I like to wear.
Orange is the orange that I like to eat.

**Luke Malkin (8)**
Glenmead Primary School

# My Poem

Pink is the bag swaying on my back.
Pink is the paint splodging on my paper.
Pink is the sunset slowly lowering from the sky.
Pink is the pig rolling happily in the mud.

Orange is the mango that slices in half.
Orange is the mane of a roaring lion.
Orange is the toothbrush that brushes side to side.
Orange is the watch that fastens to my wrist.

Red is a strawberry that is made to squash.
Red is the pencil that glides on my page.
Red are the lips moving up and down.
Red is the book that sways open.

Yellow is the sun that sets from the sky.
Yellow are the petals that grow to a flower.
Yellow is the ruler that makes a straight line.
Yellow are the stars that dance in the sky.

**Laura Bicknell (9)**
Glenmead Primary School

# Blue, Red And Silver

Blue is the bright sea making waves on the beach.
Blue is the high sky, light and bright.
Blue is the big pot that pens and pencils are put into.

Red is my wallpaper in the shop.
Red is a sports car zooming down the streets.
Red is a fire extinguisher that puts out fires.
Red is a pot that things go into.

Silver are the stars shining in the sky.
Silver is the moon, making it night.
Silver is the money you buy with.

**Dean Morgan (9)**
Glenmead Primary School

# My Colour Poem

Red is the romantic
Valentine's of a rose.
Romantic people
Would love to have one.

Orange is the
Glowing of the sun
Burning away
And making things light.

Yellow is the
Bitterness of a lemon.
When the sourness of
The lemon touches my tongue
It makes me tingle.

Green is the
Emerald of grass
Swaying in the breeze.

**Rachael Finnerty  (9)**
Glenmead Primary School

# My Sweet Poem

Red is my cover keeping me safe and comfortable.
Red is the sunset shining by me.
Red is berries, soft with seeds.
Red is earrings that brighten you up.
Orange is a radiator that I can turn on.
Orange is my teddy that I snuggle up to.
Orange is an orange that is juicy and sweet.
Orange is marigolds that smell nice with pollen.
Blue is a bluebird that tweets in the morning.
Blue is like glasses that let people see.
Blue is the sky that keeps me warm.

**Meena Ali  (8)**
Glenmead Primary School

# My Colour Poem

Blue is the pupil of the eye,
Putting colour in the seas and sky.

Red is the romance of the rose
That brings love around.

Orange is the glow of the sun
Burning away to make things bright.

Yellow is the roundness of Winnie the Pooh,
Soft and cuddly like fluff.

Green is the brightness of grass,
Big and strong, that stands nice and tall.

White is the stickiness of glue,
You stick it on things.

**Renée Blissett  (8)**
**Glenmead Primary School**


# Colours

Green is my Lamborghini racing quickly down the road.
Green is a leaf as light as a feather falling softly in the breeze.
Green is a pointed blade of grass swaying in the wind.
Green is a grape, squashed to make wine.

Red is the flame of a burning fire in the breeze.
Red is an apple in the summer sun.
Red is a strawberry, juicy and sweet.

Yellow is a sunflower moving in the breeze.
Yellow is the sun rising up into the sky.
Yellow is a lemon, sour and bright.

**Thomas Lissemore  (9)**
**Glenmead Primary School**

# My Rainbow

Red is the romance of a rose showing who you love.
Orange is the seed of the peach, biting through the juicy flesh.
Yellow is the light of the sun beaming down towards us to give
us light.
Green is the brightness of a cricket pitch with England winning the
World Cup.
Blue is the glistening of a calm sea swaying side to side.
Indigo is the water of the swimming pool heated up by the sun.

**James Ricketts (9)**
Glenmead Primary School


# Colours

Orange is the colour of smelly old socks that my mum wants me
to wear.
Orange is the colour of the shining new coat that I wear all the time.
Orange is the colour of a dusty old ball that I play with.
Red is the colour of the new beautiful paper that we decorate with.
Red is the colour of the beautiful shining crayon that I colour with.
Red is the colour of fresh, sweet strawberries that I like.

**Simon Eccles (8)**
Glenmead Primary School


# Part Of The Rainbow

Blue is the waves of the sea waving away free.
Blue is the light of the sky making the clouds go by.
Blue is the shining of eyes making us happy.
Red is the light of Mars, and I don't mean chocolate bars.
Red is the rushing of a fire engine speeding away to the rescue.
Green is the shade of the leaves falling off the trees.

**Reiss Munslow (8)**
Glenmead Primary School

# The Future

What will be
Left here for me
When I grow up?

Will there be
Rubbish bins
To put rubbish in?

Will factories
Rule most
Of the world?

Will there be
Animals for meat?
Or cows and goats for milk?

Will there be
Too much pollution
To see the sun?

Will there be
Fish in the sea
For us to eat?

Will we have
Anything left
To look at?

**Callum Ward  (8)**
**Glenmead Primary School**


# My Poem

Blue is the sun blooming against my face,
Blue is a woman's scarf flowing in the air.

Green is a plant's stem playing around,
Green is a juicy apple being eaten, sweet and wide.

Yellow is the sun brightening up the beautiful sky,
Yellow is a lemon to make lemon juice for pancake day.

**Ronan Sheehan  (8)**
**Glenmead Primary School**

# Rainbow Poem

Red is the
Heart of a fire
Gleaming with brightness.
Red is the
Juicy taste of strawberries
In a glass bowl.
Red is the
Glistening look of
The sunset going.

Orange is the
Light of the sun
Going away and
Keeping things light.
Orange is the
Juicy taste of fruit tasting lovely.
Orange is the
Glowing of the sun
Glistening in the light.

Yellow is the
Sweet kind of fruit
That makes me go, 'Ah, sweet.'
Yellow is the
Glowing of the sand
When I touch it,
It is so soft.
Yellow is the
Brightness of the sun
Standing in the wind.

**Demi Roberts (8)**
**Glenmead Primary School**

# My Grandma

My grandma loves toffee,
But not more than coffee.

My grandma hates splinters,
But not more than winters.

My grandma loves me,
But she's got a bad knee.

My grandma loves dates,
But hates to clean the plates.

**Callum Gander  (9)**
Glenmead Primary School

# Spring

Beautiful pink flowers growing in lovely green, green grass.
Green trees blowing in the wind.
Birds singing as they make a nest.
Trees rustling as the wind blows against them.
Fresh flowers as they open up.
Rain as it drops on me.
Rain as it drops on my tongue.
Happy and excited for spring.

**Caitlan Hall  (7)**
Hawkesley Church Primary School

# Spring

I see birds nesting again.
I hear bees buzzing in the flowers.
I smell blossoms on the trees and daffodils.
I feel the wind blowing my bike.
I taste my birthday cake.
Happy and excited spring is here!

**Deanna Arlington  (8)**
Hawkesley Church Primary School

# Spring

Lovely colourful flowers in the shiny green grass.
Beautiful lambs munching the fields.
Birds whistling as they sing in the morning.
The wind blowing on the windowpane.
Perfume of pretty flowers like tulips and daffodils.
Smell of fresh air.
The heat of the sun.
The soft rain.
Tasty birthday cake and lemony pancakes.
I am grateful that spring is here.

**Rebekah Hare (8)**
**Hawkesley Church Primary School**


# Spring

Shining leaves blowing in the breeze.
A herd of clouds gathering.
Birds pecking on the tree.
Strong wind whistling.
Perfumed flowers.
Fresh grass.
Ice melting.
Warmer days.
Longer days.
Rain on my tongue.
Spring is exciting.

**Kalum McCrea (8)**
**Hawkesley Church Primary School**


# Spring

Bees buzzing around the hive.
Smell of blossom.
Warm sun on my face.
I am happy in the spring.

**Chantelle Quinn (8)**
**Hawkesley Church Primary School**

## My Parrot, Mykey

P arrots are nice, furry like mice
A bout at night, around the light
R ound the corners
R eady to squawk
O n the lamp post hanging like a bat
T ail so red, like a volcano
S o watch out, Mykey's about.
    He could bite your head off in a shout.

**Jodie Chandler  (9)**
Hawkesley Church Primary School

## The Wind

The wind is blowing in my hair,
Leaves are flying everywhere.
How I wish I could be inside,
Where I could sit, be warm and hide.
I'm sitting outside my tall, tall tower,
The wind is going 30 miles per hour.
I could be warm but I chose to be cold,
The wind can kill, so I've been told.

**Lauren Robertson  (10)**
Hawkesley Church Primary School

## Seasons

S easons are like flowers
E ven if they're cold
A mazing, beautiful colours
S urround living things
O verall I like summer
N o seasons bother me
S o watch out, seasons are about!

**Michael Henderson  (9)**
Hawkesley Church Primary School

# Best Friends

B est friends stick together
E veryone together
S ometimes they disagree
T wo games they play

F riends forever
R eally kind
I n their hearts
E ven when they go stomping off
N ever be too shy
D efinitely to your friends
S tay with your friends when they're there.

**Kayleigh Shirley  (9)**
**Hawkesley Church Primary School**


# Spring

Beautiful pink flowers growing in the grass.
Birds singing in the trees.
Perfume of pretty flowers in the grass.
Rain drips on me.
I am pleased that spring is here.

**Kaleigh Astbury  (7)**
**Hawkesley Church Primary School**


# Spring

I see blossoms glowing in the sun.
I hear birds singing in their nests.
I smell crocuses under the trees.
I feel the wind blowing around me.
I taste my pancakes.

**Usmaan Ali  (9)**
**Hawkesley Church Primary School**

# I Hate The Rain

I just want to go out to play,
But it's been raining all day,
But my mum said I'll get wet, I don't care.
I don't care if I wreck my hair
I'll put my boots on and my coat.
I want to get wet,
Get wet just like a boat.
I can hear the raindrops spitter-spatter,
On the ground pitter-patter.
That's the rain.

**Charity Bravington  (9)**
**Hawkesley Church Primary School**


# Spring

Trees blowing in the wind.
Children shouting as
They play outside.
Wind blowing.
Taste of birthday cake.
I am excited that spring is here!

**Chloe Butcher  (8)**
**Hawkesley Church Primary School**


# Spring

Glowing ice melting.
Birds singing in the nest.
Perfume of beautiful bluebells.
Wind blowing on me.
Taste of raindrops on my tongue.
I am excited to know that spring is here.

**Chloe Welsh  (8)**
**Hawkesley Church Primary School**

# The Wind

The wind, it slams against the window,
I can't get to sleep.
It slams the door, it annoys us.
The wind, it blows the trees and branches break.
It makes me angry.
It whacks the branches against my window,
It makes me go mad.
The wind annoys me. Can you just stop?
You really are annoying me.
Do you like the wind?

**Jade Sykes  (10)**
**Hawkesley Church Primary School**


# Spring

A herd of clouds gathering.
Puddles bubbling.
Raindrops splashing on the ground.
The scent of minty flowers.
Warmth of the sun.
Delicious pancakes.
Happy and joyful spring.

**Liam Fendick  (9)**
**Hawkesley Church Primary School**


# Spring

I see leaves blowing in the wind.
I hear birds singing in their nests.
I smell the wet grass.
I taste the lovely taste of pancakes.
I am grateful that spring is here.

**Nayer Caesar  (7)**
**Hawkesley Church Primary School**

# Windy Times

The wind is blowing on the roof.
All the wind does is sneeze all night, all night.
The drawers are slamming all the time.
The wind is blowing night by night.
The wind always blows, it's really, really cold,
It makes me feel bold.
My coat hood is tapping, all from the wind,
My feet have frozen, all from the wind,
My cat has frozen, all from the wind.

**Joshua Harrington (9)**
Hawkesley Church Primary School


# A Windy Day

The wind is blowing people back,
It drives people crazy.
People's clothes are blowing up,
The wind is gushing side to side
And swaying side to side.
The wind is crashing together,
I can hear whistling when
The trees are swaying.

**Chloe Smith (10)**
Hawkesley Church Primary School


# Spring

I see blossoms glowing in the sun,
I hear birds singing in their nests,
I smell crocuses under the trees,
I feel the wind blowing around me,
I taste my pancakes.

**Hannah Horton (8)**
Hawkesley Church Primary School

# The Wind

The wind blows everywhere.
It blows the leaves,
It rustles my hair.
You can't see it,
But you can hear it.
It rushes at eight miles per hour,
That's what I've been told.
It whacks your house windows
Like a mad person trying to get you,
So you lock yourself up
And you're safe.
The wind blows everywhere.

**Sian Kelly (10)**
**Hawkesley Church Primary School**


# Spring

Beautiful flowers growing.
Baby ducklings following their mum.
Robins pecking in the tree.
Smell of blossoms on the tree.
I am happy in spring.

**Rebecca Wincott (8)**
**Hawkesley Church Primary School**


# Spring

The leaves grow in the spring.
The flowers say in the sun,
Spring has just begun.
Butterflies start flying in the spring.
Rabbits start hopping in the spring.
Happy and joyful spring.

**Dean Hensey (9)**
**Hawkesley Church Primary School**

# It's A Windy Day Today

It's a windy day today,
I hear the wind puff and buff,
Windows crashing, dustbins bashing,
Doors slamming.
I don't like the wind, do you?
Creaking floors and bashing doors,
Snapping trees and rattling keys.
I don't like the wind.

**Chloe Jones (10)**
Hawkesley Church Primary School

# Windy Day

The trees swaying in the breeze,
Wind whistling through my bedroom window,
Hear it hammering on the roof,
Feels so cold

Then it slows down,
Not so cold,
Not so hard,
Then it stops . . .

**Paige Britton (9)**
Hawkesley Church Primary School

# The Wind

The wind it blows,
The wind it sighs,
The wind it comes down from the skies.
It huffs and puffs,
So go away wind
And leave me alone!

**Shelby Barrington-Smith (10)**
Hawkesley Church Primary School

# The Wind

I'm standing outside,
What do I hear?
Creaky trees,
Whispering leaves,
Windy breeze.
It's grey and gloomy,
Dark and dim.

I'm standing outside,
What do I see?
I see branches
Sweeping to me,
Grass swaying side to side,
Litter clattering
By my side.
This never stopped
Until it was late.

Do you like the wind?

**Remi Graham (9)**
Hawkesley Church Primary School


# I Hate The Wind

I'm standing outside with the wind all around me,
It's blowing me to and fro,
I'm shaking to death with the wind in my face,
Wrapping my coat around me and I wish it would surely go.
The wind tries to talk to me but I just ignore it,
Then it gets mad and gets a bit bad,
I'm hoping it will surely go away.
I hate it when the wind plays knock-door-run,
So when I go to answer, it thinks it's rather fun.
So when I go to get it, it just runs away,
So all it wants to do is run and play.
There's one thing I like, it's when it goes away,
So when I go to bed I've had a brilliant day.

**Kyanne Brookes (10)**
Hawkesley Church Primary School

# The Wind

It was a drab, gloomy morning,
Quite close to dawning.
I went to the shop
And then I saw it.
It danced in circles,
Twirling and circling,
And then . . .
I felt it, powerful.
It was trying to make
Me stay still but I pushed,
I cuddled myself up in my coat
Then I smelt it . . .
I smelt the cold and
The smell of the countryside.
And then I heard it.
I heard it go as silent as a mouse,
The wind went to sleep.

**Yasmin Harvey  (9)**
**Hawkesley Church Primary School**


# Windy Day

Windy day, windy day,
What am I going to do?
I'm going to clatter, crash, scurry
And flutter you.
So windy day, windy day,
Leave me alone
And wait until I get home.

Windy day, windy day,
What am I going to do?
I'm going to tickle your toes,
Open the windows, let the wind through
And now I'm going to torture you.
So windy day, windy day,
Go back home.

**Amy Coggins  (10)**
**Hawkesley Church Primary School**

# The Windy Days

The wind is crashing on my windows,
The wind is dancing like mad,
The wind is blowing on my bare head,
The wind is blowing the peaceful grass,
The wind is blowing on my football.

The wind is blowing,
The trees are crying,
The doors are slamming.

Cracking cans, slamming doors,
The branches are sad,
The neighbours are angry.

The wind has gone now,
The sun has arrived,
The trees are huffing,
My face is dry.
Thank you, so now let's . . .
*Play out!*

**Kielo Brown  (10)**
**Hawkesley Church Primary School**


# Windy Day

The wind it blows,
It blows so strong,
The wind, the wind,
It creaks so much
And when it does, I fall down,
It sounds like it's howling,
It sounds like it's roaring,
So I like chattering,
The wind likes scattering,
I hear the wind gushing from side to side,
It's pushing me a lot,
I want it to *stop!*

**Chloe Maddocks  (9)**
**Hawkesley Church Primary School**

# Stop It, Please Stop It

The day that took a moment, no longer.
Why, what who?
Why am I doing this?
What is it?
Me, I haven't done anything.
Who is this person inside of me?
As my tears of sadness went down beside me,
I could not look at myself.
Well, if I could do anything besides this,
I would stand my ground.

**Hannah Prentice  (11)**
**James Brindley Children's Hospital**


# Anger

Anger is red like fire,
It looks like a comet.
Anger sounds like a tiger roaring,
It tastes bitter like rotten eggs.
Anger smells like plastic burning
And feels like a dry hard rock.

**Angelo Evangelou  (10)**
**James Brindley Children's Hospital**


# Happiness

Happiness is pink.
Happiness looks like fun,
It sounds like birds singing,
It smells like flowers, like daffodils.
Happiness tastes like a barbecue,
It feels like fresh air.

**Millie Hodson Walker (7)**
**James Brindley Children's Hospital**

# Ten Boring Teachers

Ten boring teachers sleeping in the sunshine,
One got sunburn then there were nine.

Nine horrible teachers woke up late,
One waited at home then there were eight.

Eight bright teachers took a trip to Devon,
One got car sick then there were seven.

Seven stupid teachers teaching us tricks,
One turned invisible then there were six.

Six bossy teachers hopping in the drive,
One broke her leg then there were five.

Five mean teachers broke the law,
One went to jail then there were four.

Four messy teachers needed to wee,
One wet herself then there were three.

Three yelling teachers cooking a stew,
One put poison in it then there were two.

Two shy teachers having lots of fun,
One got over-excited then there was one.

One lonely teacher chewing a bun,
She broke all her teeth then there were none.

**Amaanat Hussain  (10)**
**James Brindley Children's Hospital**


# Shape Poem

Beautiful birds sitting in a nest as long as they can rest.
Blossom and bushy holly leaves, slimy insects and snails.
Palm trees, brown, shiny conkers. Ash, bay, green leaves, big!
Acorns, brown slimy bark. Hazel, chestnut trees.
Tamarisk, oak, green leaves, brown and orange leaves.
Sycamore, maple, rowan, spruce, willow, pine, larch, cedar.

**Mohammed Arslan  (10)**
**Leigh Junior, Infant & Nursery School**

# I'm Scared Of The Dark!

Out jumps a skeleton from my wardrobe
Under my bed
From my window
Out of my head!

Slugs and snails lurking on my pillow
On top of my blanket
Eating my homework
Inside my jacket!

Ghosts coming through walls, awakening from the dead
Floating up high
Through and out doors
Underneath floorboards!

Vampire standing, turning into a bat
Flying out of my window
Up and below
*Turn the light on!*

**Hassan Hussain  (10)**
**Leigh Junior, Infant & Nursery School**


# Quietly

Quietly
I crept downstairs.

Quietly
I read a book.

Quietly
I went downstairs.

Quietly
I drew a picture.

Quietly
I did my homework.

Quietly
*Busy!*

**Shafan Mohammed  (9)**
**Leigh Junior, Infant & Nursery School**

# My Favourite Things

Sweets that are pink and blue,
When I lick them, they stick like glue.
Diamonds, necklaces and ruby rings,
These are some of my favourite things.

Dresses that tingle and jingle like bells,
White and yellow cockle shells.
Colourful parrots with beautiful wings,
These are some of my favourite things.

**Naila Abid (10)**
**Leigh Junior, Infant & Nursery School**


# I'm Scared Of The Dark

A two-headed monster with four eyes and a very ugly face
Under my bed,
By my window,
Next to the desk,
Then by my toys
And now by me.
*Turn on the lights!*

**Tayba Nawaz (10)**
**Leigh Junior, Infant & Nursery School**


# The Scottish Young Girl

There was a young girl
Who had her hair curled.
She had one friend
Who liked to bend.
What a foolish young girl.

**Aliya Balal (9)**
**Leigh Junior, Infant & Nursery School**

# I'm Scared Of The Dark

I'm scared of the dark
Where roaming monsters
Scare me to death
I'm hiding under my bed covers
Where I shiver and shiver and shake
When I peep my head out
*Boom!*
*Boom!*
*Boom!*
Went the noise!

*I'm scared of the dark!*

**Marieh Parveen (10)**
**Leigh Junior, Infant & Nursery School**


# Seasons

Here is winter,
When the snow falls,
You will get presents
At Christmas time.

Here is spring,
When spring flowers grow,
It is nearly Easter
And the lambs are born.

Here is summer,
The time of year
Everyone is waiting for,
So get out there.

Here is autumn
When the leaves fall,
Get your coats on now
And wrap up warm.

**Amy Ellis (8)**
**Lyndon Green Junior School**

# The Girl And The Ice Cream

I saw a girl the other day,
I asked her if she
Would like to play.

She was a little mean
And said, 'No, go away,
I'm eating my ice cream.'

It was strawberry, vanilla
And chocolate.
It had sprinkles and a flake,
Just the ice cream
I would make.

I waited for her
To give me a taste,
But instead she pulled a face.

I ran off to tell
And she ran too
And she tripped and fell!

**Chloe Bond  (7)**
**Lyndon Green Junior School**


# My School

School is fun,
It is fun, fun, fun.
It is great to work,
So come to school.

School is great
And you can play,
You can play football.

The teachers are nice,
But you can get told off,
So never push your friends
And school will be
Fun, fun, fun.

**Ryan French  (9)**
**Lyndon Green Junior School**

# Bonfire Night

On Bonfire Night
You always get a fright.

On Bonfire Night
It's a lovely sight.

On Bonfire Night
The colours are lovely and bright.

On Bonfire Night
Everyone has such a lovely time.

**Joshua Preece  (9)**
Lyndon Green Junior School

# Touch, Touch

Touch, touch,
What can you feel?
The smoothness of a baby's heel.

Look, look,
What can you see?
The golden crib hanging from the sky,
She stared at the string with lovely blue eyes.

**Megan Goodwin  (8)**
Lyndon Green Junior School

# Friendship

Friendship is the colour of sky-blue,
It smells like a rose on a hot sunny day,
It tastes like a drop of your favourite drink,
It sounds like the sea on a cold winter's night,
It feels like the touch of your family's hand in the morning,
It lives in the bottom of your heart.

**Abigail Jones  (9)**
Lyndon Green Junior School

# Friendship

Friendship is the colour of perfect pink,
It smells like a rosy flower.
Friendship tastes like a beautiful sweet,
It sounds like a love heart beating,
It feels like a kiss from the one you love.
Friendship lives in the caring Heaven.

**Emma Warwood (10)**
Lyndon Green Junior School

# Friendship

Friendship is the colour of bright yellow,
It smells like daffodils blowing in the breeze,
It tastes like vanilla ice cream,
It sounds like children in the playground,
It feels good because you're having fun,
It lives in the sky, bright in the sun.

**Bethan Machray (10)**
Lyndon Green Junior School

# The Leaf

Look at the leaves
Tumbling from the trees.

Red, green, yellow, brown,
Look at them blowing into town.

Aren't they pretty, just like the branches?
Leave, oh leaves.

**Demi Baker (8)**
Lyndon Green Junior School

# Fairies At Night

Once there was a little girl,
She woke up in the night,
She saw some little fairies
And gave them all a fright.

There were blue ones and red ones
That flew around her place,
Then she said,
'Please take me to space.'

So off they went in the sky,
Then she got really scared,
So they took her down
And she got into bed.

**Isobel Wattison  (9)**
**Lyndon Green Junior School**


# Do You Want To See A Shark?

Do you want to see a shark?
OK, you must go down
To the cold, gloomy river.

I know a shark! She's mean,
She's wicked, she's a killer.

But don't stay there for too long.
Run for your life!

**Lauren Boyle  (8)**
**Lyndon Green Junior School**

# Anti-Smoking

Here lies Tommy Bun
Who thought it would be fun
To take a fag
And have a drag.

He smoked ten packs a day
Now he will never smoke again.
His clothes smelt
And his teeth were yellow.

He took one puff
I really think he smoked enough.
He started when he was five
Now that fool is not alive.

I hope you have read this poem
And hope you don't smoke
Like Tommy Bun.

**Louise Doherty  (10)**
**Oaklands Primary School**


# Plant Parts

Big and bright,
Catch me in sight.
Large and red,
I sit in a flower bed.

Long and green,
I can't be seen.
I carry up nutrients,
But not scents.

My roots keep me in the ground,
I'm the first to be found.
They carry nutrients
For the top bits.

**Aqeela Zafar  (11)**
**Oaklands Primary School**

# What I Want To Be

I'd like to be a model girl, long and lean.
I'd like to be a star, shining from the stage.

I'd like to be a poet, singing out my poems.
I'd like to be a doctor, helping and curing.

I'd like to be a dancer, twirling round.
I'd like to be a judge, thinking about them.

I'd like to be a writer, books and books.
I'd like to be a teacher, giving out homework and lectures.

I'd like to be a bully, making you cry.
I'd like to be an eater, fatter and fatter.

I'd like to be a banker, getting more money.
I'd like to be a dunce, spelling *whoz ???*

I'd like to be a queen, commanding you.
I'd like to be a god, creating peace.

I'd like to be a maker, making things.
I'd be anything, I think.

**Laura Chui  (10)**
**Oaklands Primary School**


# I Know Someone

I know someone who can
Drink milkshake from their nose.

I know someone who can
Twist their arm back on their elbow.

I know someone who can
Bend their body into a circle.

I know someone who can
Do stunts in a car, on a bike,
With their feet on their head,
And that someone is *me!*

**Sufyaan Zafar  (9)**
**Oaklands Primary School**

# Lazy Bones

Clean your room,
My mum moans,
Stop being such
A lazy bones.

Wash your face,
My dad groans,
Stop being such
A lazy bones.

I don't want to
Do anything,
Just leave those dishes
In the kitchen sink.

My room's a mess
And everyone moans,
But I don't care,
I'm a lazy bones.

**Lauren Gilligan  (9)**
**Oaklands Primary School**


# My Dog, Holly

Oh my dog, Holly,
Is such a wally,
She likes to lick my foot.
The silly mutt.
She is so big and fat,
She is sometimes mean to my cat.
She almost set her tail on fire
Because her tail is like a non-stop, moving wire.
She's got short golden-yellow hair.
Try and bite me? She wouldn't dare.
Oh my dog, Holly, is such a wally.

**Grace Verona  (9)**
**Oaklands Primary School**

# My Cat

I've got a cat,
He sleeps on the mat.
He loves to play,
But not on a rainy day.

His name is Lucky
And he likes getting mucky.
He's got small paws
With sharp claws.

He loves playing with mice,
He thinks his dinner is nice.
My cat has got green eyes,
He sometimes chases flies.

**Kathryn Hope (11)**
Oaklands Primary School

# Together

Together we stand united,
Together we stand as one,
Togetherness keeps us happy,
It's better than being alone.
It's like when animals stick together,
Some stay in packs.
Well really, our families
Are just like that.

**Sarah Keating (10)**
Oaklands Primary School

# The Sea Is A Galloping Horse

The sea is like a galloping horse
Running and galloping, using all its force
Running around sprinting and jumping
Never stopping until it's spring
Always jumping in the deep blue sea
Thinking everything in life is always free

His hooves are clattering as if he is made
Since he is lonely and is usually sad
Now it's getting louder and louder
Rain is falling, making the sea deeper and deeper
The rain is getting heavier and heavier

Months have passed, now spring is on its way
The galloping horse starts to neigh
Forgetting that he can always play
The sapphire horse is now very glad
No one is mad
Everyone can play with him.

**Alanna Ayres  (10)**
Robin Hood J&I NC School


# The Sea Is Like A Galloping Horse

Sea is like a galloping horse
Never stopping on its journey around the world
Charging around, using all its force
Disguising itself in the sapphire-blue sea

Its hooves always scraping across rocks
The land is blocked which makes him mad
Closest he can get to land is on the beach
For this part sometimes makes him glad

Months have passed, spring is here
Now he must confront his fear
But how, what, when, why?
Trapped for all eternity.

**Joshua Ryder  (10)**
Robin Hood J&I NC School

# The Sea Is A Hungry Octopus

The sea is a hungry octopus, giant and blue.
He lies around doing nothing.
He gnashes with his gritty teeth
Licking crumbling, cracking pebbles.
When the breezy wind hurls the oceans,
He leaps majestically, leaving his poisonous ink.

When the sea tide roars, he drifts to the surface floors.
He sniffs and snuffles the salt sea air,
Splitting inside his sloppy skin, his tentacles,
He screeches, hollers long and loud.

But on quiet days in March or June,
When the grass on the dune, no more greedy tunes,
With his head between his jaws he lies out in the sea,
So quiet, so long, he scarcely breathes.

**Charlotte Winder  (9)**
Robin Hood J&I NC School

# The Rainbow Is Like A Mermaid

Rainbow is like a mermaid
Colours splashing
Scales on a mermaid
Stripes on a rainbow

Swimming elegantly through the crystal-clear blue sky
Colours reflecting

Gentle breeze caresses her delicate face
Cooling her down
She searches for her pot of gold

As she floats over the river
She sheds a tear
Ripples becoming a million droplets.

**Bina Lakha  (11)**
Robin Hood J&I NC School

# The Wind Is A King

Wind is king, boisterous in dead of night,
Gusting, creating tornadoes, disruption,
Invincible.
Winter and autumn, he's stronger.
He moans and groans in his loneliness,
He is ruthless.
Watching everything in the world at the same time.
He's looking at the animals in the zoo
That are locked up and
Are stuck in their cages.
They cannot get out.
Wind always feels sorrow for them in his heart,
Is not only purely ruthless.
He thinks of his own kind constantly,
If they will be in his form and have someone to talk to.
As this creature,
The king of the jungle, a lion.

**Tahrif Khan  (10)**
**Robin Hood J&I NC School**


# The Sea Is Like A Hungry Dog

Sea is like a hungry dog, giant, grey
Thrashing in and out of waves
Howling and hollering
Gnawing on shores all day
Tumbling in and out of giant waves

Night
Shaggy dog shivers
Groans, moans
Sniffs, snuffs
Shaking his filthy coat into murky water

May, June
Dog turns calm
Head deep in his paws
Silent, not even a snore.

**Rachel Batten  (9)**
**Robin Hood J&I NC School**

# The Sea Is A Hungry Dog

The sea is a hungry dog. Giant, grey
He rolls upon hot sandy beaches all day, every day
With his ginormous clashing teeth and his enormous shaggy jaws.
Hour after hour he gnaws on rumbling, tumbling rocks and stones,
Licking his wet, huge paws.

When night wind roars like vicious dogs chasing intruders,
The moon shakes stormy, rainy clouds.
The sea-dog jumps to his feet, snuffs, sniffs,
Searching for delicious juicy prey.
Cascading his wetness all over the cliffs,
He howls and hollers long and loud day after day.

But quiet days in May and June,
When even seagulls keep calm and quiet,
With his shaggy head between his paws
He lies on the rocky shores
So silent, you scarcely hear him snore.

**Jaspreet Bhogal  (9)**
**Robin Hood J&I NC School**


# The Hurricane Is Like A Hideous Vulture!

The monstrous hurricane, a deadly element,
For the hurricane is like a hideous vulture scavenging,
Swooping, swishing to and fro,
For when the wind's gentle, it's a warm and lovely day,
Until the wind shows no mercy.

Smash, crash, bash, the monstrous wind plays with lives,
Snap, trees fall, for the wind shows no mercy like a vulture would.
People's screams fill the air with coldness and fear,
For the wind is a hurricane, nature's vacuum, also nature's toy,
For the hurricane picks up helpless souls tossing away the remains,
Acting like a vulture.

As night falls, the hurricane dies down but still lurks among the land,
For nature will come tomorrow
And be the vulture once again!

**Jack Sandall  (11)**
**Robin Hood J&I NC School**

# The Sea

The sea is a hungry shark. Giant and grey.
He lolls about doing nothing all day.
His gnashing teeth and spiky fin,
Minute by minute he gnaws,
Crumbling, crumpling stones.
Oh moans, moans, moans,
Giant sea shark bones,
Biting his only prey.

When night-time roars,
Moon rocking misty air,
He swims to shore, snuffs and sniffs,
Spitting his insides all over cliffs,
Hollers and howls, long and loud.

But on quiet days in March and May,
When even grass on dunes
Plays more greedy tunes,
His one too many prey,
He slumbers night and day,
So quiet, so long, he scarily breathes.

**Alex Phelan  (10)**
**Robin Hood J&I NC School**


# The Wind Snake

Hissing, whistles through fingers of mankind,
Coiling tornado strangles,
Attacks in venomous gales,
Hurricane rattlesnake quivering, acid bite,
Snap, snap,
Swallows, digests the diseased rat,
Blizzard tongue licking the earth
Leaving an alphabet of panic, pain,
Enamelled, shredded skin hails with colours of the rainbow.

**Joe Hinckes  (11)**
**Robin Hood J&I NC School**

# The Wind Is Like An Eagle

Soars mightily in the sky, dragging thick clouds behind.
Storm.
His prey, a village. He swoops down to catch it,
Bringing a mighty storm with him.
Demolishes everything in his path.
His talons crush the unaware creatures,
Wings slice through icy air, like blades.
He flies over, watching, spying on the ground below.
His great eyes never shut, always watching for his next opportunity.

He elegantly sways through grassy fields.
His head stands proud above all else.
Soaring up and swooping down,
His beak points ahead at full speed, like the point of a rocket.
Fanning out his tail for take off,
His streamlined body like Concorde,
Too fast for the naked eye.

**Muhammad Azarpay (11)**
**Robin Hood J&I NC School**


# Pecking Hailstones

As the hailstones come dropping from above,
All children run to their snug and welcoming houses,
But one child stays still in the cold, misty air.
Hailstones peck wildly at the youngster,
Fiercely the stones plunge down, crashing to the ground,
There is no hope for this frightened child.

The beak drums down upon the brisk rooftops,
A demolished town from what this horror has caused,
What kind of lethal thing is this?

Hailstones
Crash onto the windowpanes
But the boy is still alone.

Morning rises with a golden beaming sun,
But still, the boy is alone . . .

**Sonal Gohil (10)**
**Robin Hood J&I NC School**

# The Wind Is A Wolf

The wind is a wolf,
Slipping past, never seen,
Biting into prey,
Ruthless.

Growling at his prey,
Howling to the moon,
So quiet, so loud.

Crafty, sneaky,
Cunning, shrewd,
Sly, quick.

Leaping,
Sprinting,
Pouncing.

Never-ending,
Stopping,
Life goes on for the wolf.

**Anthony Briggs (9)**
**Robin Hood J&I NC School**


# The Sea

The sea is like galloping horses, tall, strong.
Standing proudly on the shore,
Cantering down shallow seas, heading for blazing hot sand,
Searching for its prey, hour after hour,
Tumbling, rumbling in and out of waves,
Moaning, groaning,
Bowling within the seas,
Swaying along the shores,
Eventually he brings himself to shore,
Arrives at a deep sleep,
No movement can be seen,
So still, so still.

**Sabrina Bano (10)**
**Robin Hood J&I NC School**

# The World Next Door

The floating galleon
Circling the mystical blue wizard's tower,
Waiting to pick up the singing children
Who await the bell to give its cold, never-ending chimes.

The trees as bare as plain paper,
Tall and thin,
The brown trees seem to bow down to the blue wizard's tower,
As if it is ruled by gods.

The blue wizard's tower strips trees to outlines,
As if it has the most power in the world,
Its gloomy shadow silhouetting the tall illuminated tower.

The silver snow spider cobweb
Holding up the glistening moon
With its strong beams occupying nature,
Brightening the snowy carpet.

**Haroon Gulfraz  (10)**
**Robin Hood J&I NC School**


# A Rose

Majestically blossoming from the ground
Soft, delicate, silky, cherry pink
Petals blooming into shape
Spreading its aroma into far distances

Buzzing bees surrounding it
Sucking sweet nectar out of it
Green caterpillars gradually crawling up
Onto the fresh green, stern stem
Dodging deadly thorns

The dazzling rose
Reflecting on the shimmering spring fountain
Growing little by little.

**Javeria Khan  (11)**
**Robin Hood J&I NC School**

# The Sea

The sea in the summer sun
Slowly like a lion
Quickly rushing
Up and down
Stalking all prey

Slowly as time fades
Skies grow and start to cascade
Pouncing up, roaring aloud
Jumping, attacking with vicious clouds

Clashing with the golden sand
Ripping, tearing, falling on land
Slowly demolishing everything in its path
Knows nothing of the aftermath

Yet slowly in the nice hot wind
It gently lies and slowly sings.

**Rahim Azimul  (10)**
**Robin Hood J&I NC School**

# The Feline Sun

The sun is a stormy feline cat. Huge, giant, golden.
He looks down on the Earth with
A small fiery beam on his face.
Golden whiskers burning in the blistering wind.

When summer comes, the cat pounces
Mercilessly at its prey, hunting rain, pursuing clouds.
Gentle purrs rumble from the heart of the sun.
He licks his rough, jagged, blazing paws effortlessly.

Night comes, the colossal star pitifully mews,
Sinking angrily.
When not angry, harmless.
When not peaceful, deadly.
King of the jungle and king of Earth.

**Jordan Golding  (11)**
**Robin Hood J&I NC School**

# The Sea Eagle

As the sea eagle glides the sand,
All children run for shelter.
Flapping fiercely,
Overlapping with its huge wings,
The enormous sea eagle shrieks,
Opening its full-size beak, then closing it,
Tightly.

Night fades into day,
Blazing sun beams onto the golden reflection
Of the sea eagle.
Silently, ferocious wings
Become calm, serene wings of the sea.

But still the boundless sea eagle
Roars and howls
Every night.

**Manisha Kaur (11)**
Robin Hood J&I NC School

# The Wind

The wind is like a stealthy snake
Hiding in the grass.
It slithers away swiftly,
Slithers swiftly as it waits for the right time to strike.
You can't see a snake hiding in reeds,
Nor the wind hiding in air.
Venomous vipers lick ground with their bodies,
Leaving an alphabet of panic.
As it writhes and wriggles,
Wind copies, raiding the lonely trees.
A noisy rattlesnake scans the ground,
Prowling for its unlucky prey.
Deadly bite, wind consumes the blazing sun.
Sheds his skin of ritual colours and goes to sleep
For now his day is over
But tomorrow will be a new day.

**Keval Vadukul (11)**
Robin Hood J&I NC School

# Under A Ramshackle Rainbow

An overgrown oak, dead and rotten,
Its branch as rough as sandpaper,
With a point as sharp as a knife attached to the end.
No creature dares to even set foot on it,
Knowing that they would be ensnared.

The sound of a raindrop falling,
As the smooth, silver and sparkling light glistens on the water end.
As I look through the crystal-clear water
I can see the reflection of emerald-green grass
Dazzled from a distance.

A thirsty well,
Sucking as much water as it can sponge,
A rose lies at the bottom of the well,
Drenched in rat-infested water.
A Shetland pony gallops past
As the midsummer moon rises.

**Wasim Ahmed  (11)**
Robin Hood J&I NC School

# The Hungry Elephant

The sea is a starving elephant,
Big and grey,
As big as an elephant's body,
As grey as its tough skin.
Munching on ships
As an elephant on leaves.
The sea will grow through global warming,
As an elephant grows throughout its life.
Oil pollutes the sea,
As elephants are poached.
And that is the sea,
A hungry elephant.

**Nicholas Wall  (10)**
Robin Hood J&I NC School

# Stars Are Like A Unicorn

Stars like a unicorn. Silver, shy.
She glides high above the sky
With her glossy mane and silver body.
Hour after hour she flies
Galloping through an ebony-ink sky, silhouetted in the evil night.
Prancing elegantly,
The royal star unicorn covers the sky.

When the night breeze soars in at last,
The pure white moon slowly spins
Away from the stars, leaving darkness behind.
She howls, in loneliness.

The stars start to fade,
The unicorn starts to weaken,
Night turns into day,
She disappears,
Disappears into thin air . . .

**Isidora Mazibrada (10)**
**Robin Hood J&I NC School**


# The Ravenous Rhino

The desert is a ravenous rhino
Dim, grey
Barges all day
Never in the mood to play
He hits the sand with a bang
And the sand briefly splits
As it scans for food
On cold, icy days
Sits alone and thumps heartlessly
For now just let it relax
Let the ravenous rhino rest.

**Hatim Hassanali (9)**
**Robin Hood J&I NC School**

# The Desert

Silver-winged mosquitoes hover over the desert,
Spitting cobra,
Venomous and deadly,
Flicking his tongue,
Spots his prey,
Lies in wait,
*Dash!*
Sucks his tasty morsel down,
Sand sweeping viciously into
Slit, open eyes.
Blinded, reels back in anger,
Swipes the tree,
Cutting clean.

Night.
Eyes change infra-red
Scan the surroundings desperately
For signs of movement.
Stars wheel around the sky.
Hissing and snapping,
Locates man, hunter.
Gun ready, shoots,
Deep, deep through the body.

Leaps back, it slithers behind a rock,
Ashamed and furious,
Falls into tranquility.

**Aqsa Ahmed (10)**
**Robin Hood J&I NC School**

# Ashamed

Why do we call ourselves rulers?
When all we do is rule the life killing

This world we live in
Will be no more
If we make the world
Nothing to live for.

If we look into the future,
We should be ashamed
That everything we waste
Is always right in our face.

When my school,
My class,
My world,
Comes to say to you, citizens,
That if you want to be alive,
To see the things we worked for
And strived for,
To see grandchildren
In future life,
Get off your comfy chair
To read this
And make a difference.

To show your love
Is not enough!
Time is running out!

**Katy Griffiths  (10)**
**Robin Hood J&I NC School**

# The Swamp

Silence of the swamp engulfs forest surrounding
The frog squatted on its lily pad
The only living creature alongside the murky depths
It listens
Waiting for some sound to approach
But it hears nothing
Until the silence is broken
A buzzing black dot
The poison tongue lashes out, digests
As swamp bubbles but never boils
Cold and congealing it tries to fuse with the frog
Now alerted, frog bounces from pad to pad, carefree
Naturally hops from pad to pad
Raging, musty green water rising behind
Still no worry
Frog stops, turns
Its purple thick tongue now visible
As it slowly opens and closes its giant mouth
Water has stopped moving
Cascades down and is instantly absorbed into the water
Frog responds with a loud croak that echoes
Throughout the landscape.

The frog ages
Its brittle bones with its skin sag down
No reason to live, helpless.
On the verge of death
The swamp moans
Its waters polluted
Reeds lying lifelessly on the surface.
As the swamp devours them slowly
The frog's life deteriorates
Collapses over and slowly falls onto its pad.
As the last bubble fades into the waters
No one realizes the loss to the world.

**Sam Muxlow  (11)**
**Robin Hood J&I NC School**

# The Sea Is Like A Jumping Dolphin

The sea is an endangered bottlenose dolphin thrashing, splashing,
Free for diving, jumping, turning and swerving.
She clicks and squeaks, flicks her fluke and dives.
Back and forth she swims, turning up where you least expect.
Her bluey-grey smooth skin dives into the water,
Joins a pod in search for food.
Now silent, except for the sound of
Swishing, clicks and squeaks, a calf has entered the world.
Quiet now, all is silent. No one would know a calf is here.

**Anastasia Raw (9)**
Robin Hood J&I NC School

# The Arctic

The Arctic, a vicious polar bear. Deadly and white.
Protecting his land
With his jagged teeth and blood-smeared claws
Quietly, silently he crouches
In blizzards of blazing snow.
The colossal crystal bear growls,
Savaging his silky prey.

**Dilan Chauhan (10)**
Robin Hood J&I NC School

# The Sea

Sea is a raging rhino. Dark, grey.
Storms swiftly against the fierce wind.
At the dead of night he is calm and weary,
He feels sorrow in his loneliness.
The sea is a raging rhino.

**Sam Covill (9)**
Robin Hood J&I NC School

# The Sun

The sun, king cobra,
Raises his hood majestically,
Shining rays on us all.

He slithers up and down as he pleases,
Biting those who wander in his presence for too long.
His whip-like tail shimmers like a red horizon.

As the body awakes from his deep slumber,
The moon does not hesitate to fall asleep.

He has a throne of clouds and is treated with utmost royalty.

**Vishaal Dhokiya (11)**
Robin Hood J&I NC School


# Juliet Loses Remoteo

Remoteo, Remoteo, where art thou?
I've looked on the sofa, the plant, the toy cow.

Remoteo, Remoteo, where art thy?
I've even looked in the farm's pigsty.
Oh Remoteo, Remoteo, where art thy?

Remoteo, Remoteo, where art thee?
I've even lost the fruit, kiwi.
Oh wait, oh wait, I remember where art thee,
Underneath the peach tree!
I've found thee, I've found thee,
What a wonder, spectacular pleasure to me.

**Chantelle Swain (9)**
St Catherine of Siena RC Primary School, Lee Bank

# The World War

In Flanders fields the poppies grow,
The war has started, off we go.
Aeroplanes fly overhead,
Then there's silence as if people are dead.
Girls looking for their family in a nightie dress,
Soldiers move as if playing chess.
People on the look out and go,
People injured from their heads to their toes!
Blood all over the muddy floor,
I wish I could transfer to another door!
When will the peace sign appear?
Show us the end of the war is near.
When will this stop?
In the fields people lie,
Oh why, oh why must people die?
People beg and people pray
Wondering if they will live today.
People wonder, people cry,
Wondering if they will die.
We have to leave one another,
Even if it's our own brother.
Why did this happen, 'Why me?' people say,
'Why do I have to be here today?'
I miss my family and friend,
Will this war ever end?
I might not see them ever again;
The floor is covered with people in pain.

When the war was over, poppies grew
As a symbol of respect for one another!

**Alisha Ullah (10)**
**St Catherine of Siena RC Primary School, Lee Bank**

# Anti-Bully

Bullying, bullying
Is a crime,
Bullying, bullying,
It's a waste of time.
Bullying, bullying,
I hate it so much,
Bullying, bullying,
It takes just one touch.
Bullying, bullying,
The torment, torture, names and teasing,
There's nothing I do for them that is pleasing.
Bullying, bullying
Is so foul,
Bullying, bullying,
Shall I end it right now?

**Naomi-Sarah Donaldson (9)**
St Catherine of Siena RC Primary School, Lee Bank


# Bullying Hurts

By following the bullies at school,
The girls thought it as cool,
But they became the fools.

When I was bullied
It made me feel sad,
I told my mom and dad,
They said it was bad.

It was scary telling of them all,
When I saw them the next day in the hall,
But it had to be done,
Because it was no fun.

**Laura Payne (11)**
St Catherine of Siena RC Primary School, Lee Bank

# Bullying

Bullying, bullying, they've got to stop.
Squashing sandwiches, taking pop.

Doing pranks and silly games,
Upsetting their feelings by calling names.

Making life hard for all,
Small, short, big and tall.

Bullying, bullying,
It has got to stop.
Squashing sandwiches, taking pop.

**Chanice Hepburn (10)**
St Catherine of Siena RC Primary School, Lee Bank


# The Bully

Bully, bully, scandalous,
Why bully? You may ask.
Is it because they are jealous?
Is it all just for show?
Are they a friend or a foe?
Do they bully for attention
Or is it that they want some affection?
Bully, bully, scandalous!

**Aaron Reiss Parmar (10)**
St Catherine of Siena RC Primary School, Lee Bank


# Love

Love is pink like small, delicious sweets,
It looks like a man and a woman taking each other's hands,
It smells like flowers planted in fresh, luscious green grass,
It sounds like the swishing of waves grabbing the sand,
It tastes like chocolate melting in your mouth,
It feels like the sun warming you on a winter's day,
That is what love is.

**Jamilah Mohammed (8)**
St Catherine of Siena RC Primary School, Lee Bank

# Slavery

What is slavery?
Is it just people taken two by two,
Or does it involve families and communities too?
That hope they would be spared by age twenty-two?

The chains on their feet and hands,
To the boss they're like a helpless band.,
Unwilling to go on the crowded deck,
The felt like they have a need to break
And the journey takes place
At a very rough pace.

They work in fear of the master
Who thinks they need to work faster.,
They are made to work while weak and battered,
As a result, they feel powerless and shattered.
Never again will they leave America
To go back to their real home, Africa.

**Eshe Mwilima  (10)**
**St James' CE Primary School, Handsworth**


# My World, Our World

I see, you see, we see colours.
I hear, you hear, we hear sound.
I see red, you see blue.
I hear singing, you hear talking.
I see yellow flowers, you see white.
I hear a man, you hear a woman.
That means we're unique.
But I tell you this . . .
We both smell the beautiful scents,
Hear and see the petalled flowers,
Watch the lustrous rainbow,
Whose colours sparkle in the falling rain.
I like it here and I wish to stay.

**Megan Sagal  (9)**
**St James' CE Primary School, Handsworth**

# Slavery

Life was happy and fun
Playing in the sun.
We used to run
Around the field.
My brother used to play
With his shield.
Playing and laughing
As the sun went down.

When I was captured
I thought I would die.
I asked many questions
Though my master told me lies.

The ship was dark, no way for me
To see the familiar sunlight of hope
And the warmth of being free.

**Nikita Janagil (11)**
St James' CE Primary School, Handsworth

# Going To Sleep

Gently I sleep, thinking of a land
With a beautiful fragrance
And glittering pavements that are
Full of bright colours,
Glamorous trees, breezing everywhere,
The wind in my hair.
I like it very much.
There are lots of candy sticks too.
I go to the chocolate factory every day,
Just watching chocolate being made
Fills me with wonder.
It's like watching a display of fireworks,
With lots of pleasant memories of happy days.

**Andrew McIntosh (8)**
St James' CE Primary School, Handsworth

# Slavery

Distraught with fear,
I see and feel
Colours, black and white appeal.
I feel hurt and powerless,
There is no hope,
Just hate and stress.
Feeling hungry,
Just eating scraps,
Wanting to be full
Like those rich chaps.
Tired, working all day long,
Can't wait until
The agony is gone.
Having no family
Makes you feel weak,
Desperately the love
And friendship I seek.
Only in my mind my loved ones come,
The crack of the whip
And then they're gone.

**Paul Fisher  (10)**
St James' CE Primary School, Handsworth


# The Beach

In the morning, the sun shines bright,
Seaweed and flowers, with a big yellow kite.
The golden sand flies around with silky leaves,
Picking up sounds.
At night the children, after playing all day,
Sleep away.
The owls talk and whistle about,
The plants feed,
The children shout
And after that, a new day calls them out.

**Hashim Khurram  (9)**
St James' CE Primary School, Handsworth

# Freedom

If I could touch freedom
It would feel like the calm waves of the ocean.

If I could see freedom
It would look like everybody treating everyone else as equals.

If I could hear freedom
It would sound like laughter.

If I could taste freedom
It would taste like sweet honey.

If I could smell freedom
It would smell like the sweet scent of fresh roses.

If I could speak to freedom I would say
Thank you for independence.

**Arrandeep Dhillon (10)**
St James' CE Primary School, Handsworth


# My Imaginary World

When I'm all alone,
When there's no one to phone,
I think of my imaginary world.
It's on planet Mars,
With all of the stars.
I think of all those friends I can make,
With all of those aliens
To share my fun
And come with me all the way.
Instead of sand
There's lots of red dust to play.

So that's my imaginary world.
I hope I can see my alien friends again
But for now, it's goodbye.

**Dana Fisher (8)**
St James' CE Primary School, Handsworth

# Snow!

Gentle snow dropping down,
Gleaming sunlight comes above.
A new white world to be enjoyed,
The scent of snow spread everywhere.
Fun places to be visited
And lots of things to do.
A cheerful place to be.
Different people greet away.
What a gorgeous place to me!

**Bisma Mughal  (9)**
St James' CE Primary School, Handsworth


# The Garden

Silky red, velvet roses
Falling from the sky.
A swing to sit on
And a rail to cry.
Glittering sunlight
Shining through,
Friendly animals
Visit me and you.
Shimmering stars
In the sky bright,
Fire lights my way to you.

**Jothi Najran  (9)**
St James' CE Primary School, Handsworth

# Sadness

Sadness is the colour of blue.
Sadness sounds like crying.
Sadness tastes like tears.
Sadness smells like sick.
Sadness looks like fire.
Sadness feels like rough waves.
Sadness reminds me of falling downstairs.

**Nathan Bayliss (10)**
Stirchley Community School

# Sadness

Sadness is the colour of dark, dark green.
The sound of sadness is a piece of slow music.
Sadness smells like onions.
Sadness looks like sick flowers.
Sadness feels like pepper.
Sadness reminds me of a funeral.

**Kyle Kemp (9)**
Stirchley Community School

# Sadness

Sadness is blue,
It sounds like fighting in the air,
It tastes like mouldy cheese,
It smells like polluted air,
It looks like loneliness,
It feels like torture,
It reminds me of when someone dies.

**Gary Cooper (11)**
Stirchley Community School

# Love

Love reminds me of moonlight and sparkling stars in my room.
Love tastes like creamy bubbles of melting chocolate in my mouth.
Love smells like freshly planted roses.
Love feels like a warm soft blanket around me.
Love looks like a bright room full of hearts and love and romance.
Love sounds like quiet music floating in the air.

**James Beck  (11)**
Stirchley Community School


# Sadness

Sadness sounds like someone crying.
Sadness is the colour of dark.
Sadness tastes like a mouldy apple.
Sadness smells like something burning.
Sadness looks like fear.
Sadness feels like a thorn bush.
Sadness reminds me of my bad days.

**Daniel Peel  (10)**
Stirchley Community School


# Happiness

Happiness reminds me of Drayton Manor.
Happiness tastes like ice cream.
Happiness looks like I am in the park.
Happiness smells like a rose.
Happiness feels like I am on my skateboard.
Happiness sounds like my cousin singing.

**Jared Pellow  (10)**
Stirchley Community School

# Happiness

Happiness reminds me of singing birds tweeting in the daylight.
Happiness feels like the garden waiting for me to run out.
Happiness looks like my mum's wonderful smile gleaming at the sky.
Happiness smells like the barbecue sizzling like mad.
Happiness tastes like chips fresh from the oven with two hands
holding them.
Happiness sounds like screaming and splashing of the water.
Happiness is the sky blue mixed with the yellow sunshine.

**Shannon McCleary (9)**
Stirchley Community School

# Sadness

Sadness sounds like loud bombing.
Sadness tastes like hot fire.
Sadness smells like black smoke.
Sadness looks like burning flames.
Sadness feels like getting burnt.
Sadness reminds me of destruction.
The colour of sadness is flaming red.

**Abrar Chowdhury (10)**
Stirchley Community School

# Happiness

Happiness sounds like a bird singing.
Happiness tastes like gravy.
Happiness smells like flowers.
Happiness looks like a field of flowers.
Happiness feels like water.
Happiness reminds me of good times.
Happiness is yellow.

**Martin West (10)**
Stirchley Community School

# Happiness

Happiness is bright yellow.
Happiness sounds like party music.
Happiness tastes like sweet candyfloss.
Happiness smells like lavender.
Happiness looks like the sunset.
Happiness feels like soft fur on a kitten.
Happiness reminds me of the seaside.

**Emma Jones (10)**
Stirchley Community School


# Happiness

The colour of happiness is blue.
Happiness tastes like a Snickers bar.
Happiness smells like rice pudding.
Happiness looks like a big ride.
Happiness feels like freedom.
Happiness sounds like a motorbike.
Happiness reminds me of my holidays.

**Kain Aldred-Barnett (10)**
Stirchley Community School


# Happiness

Happiness sounds like a peaceful song.
Happiness tastes like juicy raisins.
Happiness smells like a flower.
Happiness looks like beautiful flowers.
Happiness feels like pure water.
Happiness reminds me of Evesham.

**John Ford (10)**
Stirchley Community School

# Happiness

Happiness feels like a soft pillow.
Happiness reminds me of parties.
Happiness looks like hugging.
Happiness smells like melted chocolate.
Happiness tastes like sweets.
Happiness sounds like playing with someone or something.
Happiness is the colour blue and green.

**Jarobi Lorenzo-Whervin (10)**
**Stirchley Community School**


# Happiness

Happiness sounds like water.
Happiness tastes like juice.
Happiness smells like the ocean.
Happiness looks like flowers.
Happiness feels like raindrops.
Happiness reminds me of shells in the sea.

**Akram Azad (10)**
**Stirchley Community School**


# Happiness

Happiness is the colour white,
It sounds like sweet music.
Happiness tastes like air,
It smells like perfume.
Happiness looks like still water
And feels like marshmallows.
It reminds me of love.

**Sam Tanner (9)**
**Stirchley Community School**

# Happiness

It sounds like children laughing,
It looks like chocolate melting,
It tastes like melted chocolate running smoothly down my throat.
Its colour is pink,
It smells like strawberries,
It feels like the warm sun shining on me.
It reminds me of fun holidays with friends and family.

**Hollie Shakespeare (11)**
Stirchley Community School

# Happiness

Happiness is the colour pink.
Happiness sounds like people making friends.
Happiness tastes like chocolate.
Happiness smells like your favourite flower.
Happiness looks like the sun.
Happiness feels like a bubble bath.
Happiness reminds me of when I am with my friend and family
And having a good time with them.

**Bethany Caldicott (10)**
Stirchley Community School

# Happiness

Happiness is the colour of light yellow.
Happiness sounds like laughter.
Happiness tastes like ice cream on a hot day.
Happiness smells like sweet sweets.
Happiness looks like people having fun.
Happiness feels smooth and calm.
Happiness reminds me about family and friends.

**Monica Gregory (10)**
Stirchley Community School

# Love

Love is the colour of the moonlit night,
It sounds like champagne fizzing when you pop the cork,
It tastes like chocolate melting in your mouth with a lovely aftertaste,
It smells like the wind blowing fresh air in your face,
It looks like the big bright sun glowing in your face,
It feels like confetti drizzling down your face.
It reminds me of all the strawberries in the shop.

**Tiar Baxter  (10)**
Stirchley Community School


# Love

Love's colour is red.
Love's sound is calm.
Love's taste is sweet as honey.
Love's smell is chocolate.
Love's look is bright blue.
Love's feel is romantic.
Love reminds you of happiness.

**Martin Frankland  (10)**
Stirchley Community School


# Love

The colour of love is pink.
Love sounds like romantic music.
Love smells like a fresh rose in a field.
Love tastes like champagne.
Love feels like you have just been born.
Love looks like a bed of roses.
Love reminds me of Valentine's Day.

**Toby Traylen  (10)**
Stirchley Community School

# Love

Love is the colour of red velvet.
Love sounds like romantic music.
Love tastes like hot chocolate.
Love smells like some rose petals being scattered around the bed.
Love looks like a lot of hearts surrounding me.
Love feels like a warm and soft hand.
Love reminds me of my first kiss.

**Leah Chitiyo (11)**
Stirchley Community School

# Love

Love is the colour of red.
Love sounds like two little birds singing.
Love tastes like minty chocolate.
Love smells like pretty roses.
Love looks like hearts.
Love feels like bubbles going pop.
Love reminds me of people dancing.

**Amy McWilliams (10)**
Stirchley Community School

# Love

It sounds like a dove chirping,
It tastes like a luxurious cherry,
It smells like a bouquet of sweet flowers,
It looks like the gates of Heaven,
It feels like a cat's soft fur.
Love reminds me of Romeo and Juliet.
Love is the colour of pink.
Love is love.

**George Garvie (11)**
Stirchley Community School

# Love

The colour of love is red,
It sounds like romantic music,
It tastes like Christmas dinner
And it smells like raining chocolate.
It looks like your favourite food,
It feels like you have been empowered
And last, it reminds me of being kissed on the cheeks.

**Shaun Caldicott  (10)**
**Stirchley Community School**


# Love

It sounds like slow, romantic music.
It feels soft and silky.
Its colour is pink and red.
It tastes like champagne.
It looks like pink and red swirling in the air.
It smells like creamy and bubbly chocolate.
It reminds me of the sparkling night sky
With golden twinkling stars that are shiny.

**Idei Durose  (10)**
**Stirchley Community School**


# Love

Pink is the colour of love.
Love sounds like sweet talk.
Champagne tastes like love.
Love smells like a joss stick burning.
Love looks like a rose.
Love feels like a warm feeling.
A heart reminds me of love.

**Nicole Evans  (9)**
**Stirchley Community School**

# Sadness

The colour of sadness is white.
Sadness is white because white is blank
And I am alone with no one around me.
Sadness tastes like me eating toast without butter
Because I am the toast and
The butter was meant to be the friends I used to play with.
Sadness sounds like people walking away
Who were meant to be my friends.
Sadness smells like lilies at the funeral of a friend.
Sadness looks like a blank page with a little dot in the middle,
The little dot is me sitting alone.
Sadness feels like people pretending to be your friends
And then they just let you down.
Sadness reminds me of walking on a path alone.

**Aqeelah Ali  (10)**
Stirchley Community School


# My Dog

My dog belongs to only me,
Well and my brother, little Danny.
Her head looks like a small hairbrush,
She's lazy, smelly and fat.

If I shout, 'Here girl,' she walks the other way,
And if I throw a stick or ball,
She flops herself down on the grass.

When she hears me filling her bowl,
She runs towards me but runs into the door.
I laugh my head off.
She jumps up and down and runs around and around.

At night she sneaks onto my bed,
In the morning I wake up to find her asleep on my head!

**Jade Griffiths  (10)**
Topcliffe J&I School

# Fairies

How far and wide the fairies fly
On a bright and golden wing,
But when they settle down to sleep,
A gentle song they sing.
Sweet queen of night,
Soft silver stars,
We're glad you're so near.

We seek our beds,
We rest our heads
Without a moment's fear.
On thistledown,
In hidden nooks,
We watch the warning light.
The joys of sleep
Upon us creep,
We wish you all goodnight.

**Laura Green (11)**
Topcliffe J&I School


# Dancing

Dancing is all I could ever think of,
You gracefully prance all around,
Cheerfully smiling and giggling aloud,
Wearing a costume makes me feel proud.
The lights dim low, the curtains are drawn,
I wait in the wing all nervous and ready to perform.
I glide on the stage, the spotlight's on me,
Who will have the chance to dance with me?
Applause from the crowd
As I leap into the air,
I land on the floor
And pirouette around.
The light's on me while I do my bow.

**Hannah Jones (10)**
Topcliffe J&I School

# Girls

Make-up, glamour and big, *bold* shoes
Are all good things girls love to use!

All the sparkles of the jewellery
Will light up faces
That might be gloomy!

Pink and fluffy, black and goth,
All these styles make these girls rock!

Singing, dancing, dreams coming true,
Are all good things that girls love to do!

Girls just having lots of fun
The best way they can.
Screaming, shouting,
Making lots of noise
To get attention from the boys!

**Annemarie Johnson (10)**
**Topcliffe J&I School**


# Seasons

S is for the sun sparkling in the summer
E is for the ever changing temperatures
A is for the autumn wind blowing leaves from trees
S is for snow drifting down in winter
O is for old leaves drying out on the floor
N is for never-ending rain through the autumn nights
S is for seeing blossom bloom in spring.

**Ellie O'Brien (9)**
**Topcliffe J&I School**

# ASD

ASD children feel very sad
Because other children make us look bad.
We get left alone, while other children play,
We feel like we have been stuffed in hay.
Some children just stare and stare at us.
So that is just us and the way we live.

**Aimee Lee (10)**
**Topcliffe J&I School**

# The Boy From Peru

There once was a boy from Peru
Who dreamed of eating his shoe.
He woke with a fright
In the still of the night,
That silly young boy from Peru.

**Ben Selby (10)**
**Topcliffe J&I School**

# The Man From Tibet

There once was a man from Tibet
Who had the weirdest pet.
It was as blue as the sky
And it caught my eye
When his pet got caught in a net.

**Kimberley Banner (10)**
**Topcliffe J&I School**

# Watch Out!

Watch out!
There's a dragon about,
He's big and hairy
And very, very scary.
He's big and green,
He's not very clean!
Watch out!
There's a dragon about,
He's really powerful
And very colourful,
He's mysterious,
He's got red and orange fire,
He's a flyer,
So watch out!
There's a dragon about.
The dragon's lair
Is quite a scare,
*Do not* go in there.
If you dare,
You'll be *supper!*
So watch out!
There's a dragon about!

**Lauren Gillespie  (9)**
**Whitecrest Primary School**

# Dragon

Dragons are big and fierce,
They blow fire,
They can fly high above the clouds.
They have sharp claws and sharp feet.
They are green and scaly,
They are scary.
You can never see them,
They aren't alive.
Dragons are magic.

**Katie Beddows  (7)**
**Whitecrest Primary School**

# Mystical Dragon

Dragons flying here and there
In the moonlit sky,
A dragon scale in the lair,
Hiding over there.
Their dark shadows fly over the cave,
Casting darkness everywhere!

Dragons hiding gold,
Dragons lovingly old,
Unhappily, foolishly,
Dragons writing perfectly,
Slyly, slowly,
Dragons somewhere hiding!

Roars of fire,
Breathing hotness into the night,
Lighting up the shadowy sky,
Until the morning,
When light fills the sky
And the dragons fall and die!

**Lauren Middleton  (8)**
**Whitecrest Primary School**


# Dragons Fight

Dragons kill,
Dragons die,
Dragons fly,
The dragon is hot,
The dragon is fierce,
Green stripes, red-flamed fire,
Dragons roar,
Dragons have sharp nails,
Dragons are scary.

**Arjun Sangha  (8)**
**Whitecrest Primary School**

# The Dragon

Smoke like mist
Fire with colours so powerful
Spikes like thorns

Strong like steel
Guarding the treasure of his master
Down in a cave with walls of stone

Scales like armour, black and orange
Fire like lava
Centuries old

Claws like swords
Shining with silver
Still not weak

Dragons soar
In the sunlight.

**Hema Moor (7)**
**Whitecrest Primary School**


# Fierce Dragon

Flames come from my mouth
Spikes go up my back
I'm mean, as mean as mean can be
Huge and terrifying
Mean and green
Like a mean machine
Breathing fire like you've never seen
Hiding in the bushes I await my prey
As I'm sniffing away
Late at night
When the moon is shining bright
I breathe fire to my heart's delight
Barbecuing everyone in sight.

**Eleanor Kumar (8)**
**Whitecrest Primary School**

# Dragon!

I'm mythical and scaly
I can fly very high
You see me as a shadow
When I swoop down from the sky

I can be as soft as a feather
I can be as heavy as a brick
I can be as fat as a stone
And I can be as thin as a stick

My claws are sharp
My colour is gold
My tail is thick
And my age is old

I eat the food
People roll in wagons
Can you guess who I am?
I'm a dragon!

**Libby Randall (7)**
**Whitecrest Primary School**


# Dragon Eyes!

Dragon eyes
Dragon flies
I can tell you just don't lie

Gold and bright
Flying in the night

Why do you cry
And lie at the same time?

My golden tears fall on the ground
*Bang, bang*
As I watch the big scaly dragon die.

**Chloe Pickard (9)**
**Whitecrest Primary School**

# Volcano!

A volcano is a colossal, tyrannical demon.
One minute it is snoozing peacefully,
But the next . . .
There is a horrendous *bang!*
The once sleeping demon bursts with incredible rage,
Detonating with fire, it annihilates all that lies before it.
Death is this merciless demon's middle name.
Lava tears down from the mountain summit at a tremendous speed,
The pure evil demolishes life as we know it.
The creature from Hell turns bodies to bright red blood
And stones and rocks to dark, hovering ash.
Step by step, people and animals alike are defenceless
Against the wrath of the terrible, indestructible beast,
Laughing deeply and smirking evilly
As it speeds through the city,
Devastating humankind.
But suddenly,
Stopping bit by bit,
It falls into a deep slumber.
The whole world breathes a sigh of relief
But they know it will take place again.
Some day . . .
The creator of torture will strike again!

**Max Purcell-Burrows (11)**
Whitecrest Primary School


# Dragon

A very big dragon
Is a big dragon indeed
He blows the shop up
Come to me, I'll blow my fire
You are small, I'm big
I stepped on you
I won't blow you
But if you pull my tail I won't blow fire.

**Coral Hatfield (9)**
Whitecrest Primary School

# Volcano

It lays in wait, the cowardly dog,
As it meekly sleeps in the black and white fog.
The canine creature grumbles and mumbles,
Possessed and grey,
He rumbles all day.

At that moment it bubbles and boils,
It spits out lava in jet-black coils.
The black-souled companion groans and moans,
Annihilation and then detonation,
Extinction throughout the whole nation!

As lava cascades down the hill,
Even the sea will get its fill,
From bones to dust,
Do what you must,
The slaughter can last all day.

The being from Hell gives out a fulfilled smirk
And then the pain-inflicting entity splutters
And savours a demonic smile,
And just then he's back to sleep.

He breaks the ultimate urn
And reveals everything is covered
With a blanket of smouldering torture!

**Rhys Williams  (11)**
**Whitecrest Primary School**


# Dragons

Some dragons are nice,
Some dragons are fierce,
Some are powerful,
Some are weak,
Some are colourful
And some are not.
Some are bright
And some are dull.

**Owen Morris  (7)**
**Whitecrest Primary School**

# Volcano

The volcano is a slumbering lion,
Snoring gently as it goes on sleeping.
This is amazing, a lion so calm and dreaming sweetly.
Suddenly, the treacherous lion awakes,
The ferocious cat sneezes, spitting out lava
And melting the floor,
Turning it from freezing cold to scorching hot.
The lion starts to roam around,
Racing from street to street,
Lashing out wherever he can,
Separating streets from towns,
Leaving nothing in his trail.
Soon a big grin spreads across his face,
The angry predator is annihilating people's innocent souls!
The evil lion is treacherous to all humans.
The evil animal trips over, falling to the ground.
The ground was the softest, comfiest bed.
The young relaxed lion gradually falls to sleep
With a gentle snore . . . zzz,
But no one knows when it will awake!
So keep away!

**Brittany Cox  (9)**
Whitecrest Primary School


# Dragon In A Castle

A dragon lives in a castle,
With fire coming from its mouth,
Scaring people as they pass from the castle,
With sharp claws and a long tail,
As long as a train and as big as a house
And never eat again,
Trying to catch people as they pass,
Running behind them to eat them alive.
People diving, people screaming and running wild.

**Jagjit Padham  (9)**
Whitecrest Primary School

# Volcano

The volcano is a soundless, slumbering dragon,
Colossal and red.
Gaining power, he bubbles to the mouth of his home.
Stretching out, he destroys all things in his path.
Suddenly he is awake and furious,
Smoke billows around his head.
The fire-breathing demon pours murderous lava down the mountain.
Annihilating all, he roars like thunder.
Faster than light,
The scaly creature rips out people's souls.
Showing no mercy, he changes bodies to blood.
His rumble of laughter echoes around the ruins of the village.
The demon slows down, stretching and yawning.
He crashes down his head, moving buildings.
The pain-inflicting predator covers himself in a blanket of ash,
Surrounded by blood, he gently snores,
Settling down for another long 100 years,
As the people left in the derelict village
Sob in despair.

**Saprina Moor (11)**
Whitecrest Primary School

# The Dragon

Dragon, dragon,
Like a bat flies so high,
Like he could never die.
His fire is very hot,
Like a big cooking pot.

He has a long tail,
Sharp claws
And very sharp teeth,
Like he could eat
A big juicy meat!

**Emma Barker (8)**
Whitecrest Primary School

# Volcano

The volcano is a sleeping tiger,
Orange and black.
Like the sun rising, he rises from his slumber,
Wake and upright,
Scanning the horizon for prey;
Prowling through the jungle,
Claws scratching,
Eyes staring.
The wrath of the tiger is on its way,
Bursting with fury, the phenomenon dashes,
Annihilating everything in his path.
As fast as lightning, the supersonic blur
Speeds through the jungle,
Leaving a trail of dust behind him.
Gradually stopping bit by bit, the creature slows down.
Dedication to destroy is demolished and . . .
Magnificently, slowly, he drifts to sleep.

**Cara Harrigan  (10)**
**Whitecrest Primary School**


# Dragon

Green dragon,
Spiky back,
Red fire,
*It sounds like a crack!*

Sharp claws,
Long tail,
Teeth stick out like a long train rail.

His breast all colours,
Flames are hot,
But not as much as . . . *lava.*

**Thomas Aston  (7)**
**Whitecrest Primary School**

# Volcano

The volcano is a calm, peaceful, sleeping cat.
Gradually he awakes,
Moaning and groaning.
Suddenly! The black-hearted cat awakes,
Rousing with an ear-piercing rumble,
Spitting like a camel,
A red and black blanket across the city.
The gigantic holy terror
Lashed out his demonic lava.
In every footstep
He snatched the soul out of innocent people,
Cooking animals for his amusement.
Once annihilated the city.
Calmly,
Peacefully,
After all his fun,
Slowly, steadily,
The big cat falls into an intense sleep,
With the scorching sun rising from the clouds.
A big sigh of relief!
But a tremendous, dreadful worry lies ahead . . .

**Katie Lunn  (10)**
**Whitecrest Primary School**

# A Dragon

I am a dragon,
I breathe hot fire,
I puff smoke,
I fly around in the air,
Like I don't care.
I have a cave,
I am very brave,
Braver than the rest,
I am a dragon.

**Jake Wood  (8)**
**Whitecrest Primary School**

# Dragon Mist

Dragon mist and eyes
Glare at you
With their golden eyes.

You see a puff
Of fiery fire,
You think it's
Your heart's desire.

But wait, you look,
You see a pair
Of big red demon's eyes.

**Thomas Farr  (8)**
Whitecrest Primary School

# The Dragon

Dragon flies,
It dies.
Yellow fire with goldy-red,
Spiky back, what else?

Green body,
Claws like swords,
Where's the wings?
On the back.

**Harry Watts  (8)**
Whitecrest Primary School

# The Boogy Dragon

He is a cool dragon,
A cool dude dressed in red
And eats people for his Ready Brek.
He dances by the moon to his favourite tune.
Hey there dragon, boogie-woogie dragon,
Hey boogie dragon, come and boogie-woogie with me.

**Gurdylan Sanghera  (8)**
Whitecrest Primary School

# Volcano

A peaceful volcano is a sleeping lion.
The sun rises over him and he slowly awakes.
A deafening roar awakes the whole jungle.
The dangerous animal runs as fast as he can around the jungle,
He crossly stomps to and fro.
*Death* approaches poor innocent animals' minds.
The predator gets so angry he goes burning red-hot.
The burning creature burns everything around him.
An enjoyable smirk travels across his face
As he demolishes things in his way.
The burning lion slowly becomes very tired
And travels back to his den.
The evil creature slowly settles down to sleep.
At that moment *life* is going through glad animals' minds.

**Leigh Burton  (9)**
Whitecrest Primary School


# Volcano

The volcano is a sleeping dragon.
Silent echoes haunt the mountain.
Suddenly, bubbles of molten lava erupt from the beast's mouth,
Death awaits the helpless villagers
At the hands of the fire-breathing dragon.
The dragon begins his curse of lava,
Showing no mercy.

The vicious, black-souled demon escapes from his deadly prism,
The lava drips out of the dragon's mouth like blood.
The dragon enjoys his annihilation,
Ripping the villagers limb from limb.
Trees bash.
In a flash of lightning the curse ends.
The dragon drifts back to his fleshy prism.
The dragon falls into a deep, deep sleep.

**Gabriel Bradnick  (9)**
Whitecrest Primary School

# Volcano

The ancient volcano is a drowsy, drunk dragon,
Colossal and red,
About to come out of bed.
A glamorous deer comes past,
The angry fire-breathing monster wakes up fast.
The demon explodes,
He rips the deer's soul out!
The scorching hot, ruby-red lava
Travels through the magnificent, beautiful valley,
Annihilating everything in sight!
A horrid, evil smile spreads across his powerful face.
He slowly, gracefully starts to close his cursed eyes!
All that destruction!
The world gives a sigh of relief.

**Matthew Watt  (10)**
Whitecrest Primary School


# Volcano

The volcano is a snoring, slumbering cat,
With his red and black coat.
Suddenly, the black-hearted predator
Begins to stir,
*Explodes!*
Spitting like a lemur, lashing out,
He makes his way to the tropical green jungle.

Showing no mercy, the humungous creature from Hell,
Annihilating the lives of innocent creatures,
Robs their black-hearted souls,
Making the jungle and animals extinct.
He gradually drifts, bit by bit . . . back to sleep.

**Jake Simkiss  (10)**
Whitecrest Primary School

# Volcano

The volcano is a quite sleeping dragon,
Colossal and fiery-red,
Roaring with fear,
Spitting out bubbly, red-hot chunks of lava,
Annihilating people's precious homes,
Showing no mercy, ripping out souls of caring people,
Destroying everything in sight.
The black-hearted dragon is enjoying it.
The murdering dragon starts to drift off to sleep,
Drifting, drifting, drifting and drifting to sleep.
The fierce dragon is asleep for another two years.

**Lauren Manton (11)**
**Whitecrest Primary School**

# Young Writers Information

We hope you have enjoyed reading this book - and that you will continue to enjoy it in the coming years.

If you like reading and writing poetry drop us a line, or give us a call, and we'll send you a free information pack.

Alternatively if you would like to order further copies of this book or any of our other titles, then please give us a call or log onto our website at www.youngwriters.co.uk

**Young Writers Information
Remus House
Coltsfoot Drive
Peterborough
PE2 9JX**

**(01733) 890066**